THE PUZZLE FACTORY SYNDROME

To Drauen,
To the Lady with the
Healthy Heart

THE PUZZLE FACTORY SYNDROME

How THE LAWS OF THE SUBCONSCIOUS Can Make You Successful, Healthy, and Happy Today!

Tom Ray

GloTag Press

Copyright © 2003 by Tom Ray

All rights reserved. No part of this book may be reproduced in any form or by any electronic or mechanical means, including information storage and retrieval system, without permission in writing from the publisher, except by a reviewer who may quote brief passages in a review. The author and publisher assume no responsibility for errors, inaccuracies, omissions or any other inconsistency herein. Any slights against anyone or any organizations are unintentional. Published by GloTag Press, 3781 Goathill Rd., Lakehills, Texas 78063

Printed In the United States of America
Cover Design by Tom Ray
Book Design by Jason and Assoc. www.masterpix.com

www.thelawsofthesubconscious.com
www.puzzlefactorysyndrome.com
www.glotag.com

ISBN 1-932357-00-9
Library of Congress Control Number: 2003090907

GloTag Press

Publisher Cataloging-in-Publication Data

Ray, Tom
  The puzzle factory syndrome: how the laws of the subconscious can make you successful, healthy, and happy today/Tom Ray,1939—1st ed.
  p. c.m.
  LCCN 2003090907
  ISBN 1-932357-00-9 (paperback)
  1. Self-help—Psychological aspects 2. Success
  3. Health 4. Happiness   I. Title
158.1'083'-4-5-6

This publication provides the Author's opinions and neither the Publisher nor the author, Tom Ray, intends to render medical, psychological, or other professional advice with this publication.

With regards to the health of the reader or anyone else's health, the Publisher and Author strongly suggest that the reader seek the services and advice of appropriate licensed professionals.

The Publisher and Author disclaim any personal liability, loss or risk incurred as a consequence of the use and application, either directly or indirectly, of any advice, information, or methods presented in this publication.

First Edition
Copyright 2003
By Tom Ray

All rights reserved. No part of this manuscript may be reproduced (by any means) without the expressed written permission of Tom Ray.

HOW TO CONTACT THE AUTHOR

Tom Ray is available for speeches and seminars, but rarely works one-on-one, since he has closed his office at the South Texas Medical Center, in San Antonio, Texas. In special situations, he is available for private consultations.

Requests for information about his services, as well as inquiries about his availability for speeches and seminars, should be directed to the address below.

Tom Ray's Audio Cassette Tapes are available by using the Order Form at the end of this book. Additional information concerning Tom Ray's tapes and services can be found at his web site.

Web Site:
www.thepuzzlefactorysyndrome.com
www.thelawsofthesubconscious.com

TABLE OF CONTENTS

PREFACE x

FOREWORD xi

DEDICATION xii

DISCLAIMER xiii

INTRODUCTION 1

CHAPTER 1
TOM RAY'S LAWS OF THE SUBCONSCIOUS 3

CHAPTER 2
MEET THE WAGNERS 19

CHAPTER 3
THE WAGNERS DID IT 41

CHAPTER 4
STRESS IS A FEELING AND FEELINGS ARE A CHOICE 53

CHAPTER 5
PUT THE UNCOMFORTABLE PAST AWAY FOREVER 65

CHAPTER 6
A LOOK AT DEPRESSION 71

CHAPTER 7
SMOKING CAN'T KILL YOU, ... 79

CHAPTER 8
THROW THE BEAR A COOKIE 87

CHAPTER 9
TO DRINK OR NOT TO DRINK 91

CHAPTER 10
FAT IS NOT FOREVER 99

CHAPTER 11
ASTHMA BEGONE 107

CHAPTER 12
HELP CURE CANCER WITH WORDS AND THOUGHTS 113

CHAPTER 13
DO YOU HAVE KIDNEY PROBLEMS? 121

CHAPTER 14
THE PROFESSIONAL ATHLETE 125

CHAPTER 15
HYPNOSIS IN OUR EVERYDAY LIVES 131

CHAPTER 16
THE MEDIA 137

CHAPTER 17
YOU HAVE BEEN BRAINWASHED 141

CHAPTER 18
THE SUPER SALESMAN 145

CHAPTER 19
OPINION VS. EMOTION 149

CHAPTER 20
HERE'S JOHNNY...THE 'TONIGHT SHOW'
THAT ALMOST WAS 151

CHAPTER 21
THE CHILD 157

CHAPTER 22
TEENAGERS ARE PEOPLE, TOO! 159

CHAPTER 23
THE SIMPLE HANDSHAKE, PLEASE 163

CHAPTER 24
PLEASE DO NOT BOTHER ME. I AM NOT DEAD 165

CHAPTER 25
PRESCRIPTION DRUG ABUSE 169

CHAPTER 26
YOU CAN ELIMINATE PAIN AND DISEASE 171

CHAPTER 27
PARALYSIS IS NOT NECESSARY 181

CHAPTER 28
TOM RAY'S COMA THEORY 187

CHAPTER 29
THE CRIMINAL MIND 191

CHAPTER 30
PHYSICAL CHILD ABUSE 193

CHAPTER 31
MARRIAGE: A TWO-YEAR CONTRACT 199

CHAPTER 32
STUTTERING IS NOT A SPEECH PROBLEM 203

CHAPTER 33
DREAMS, DREAMS, DREAMS 207

CHAPTER 34
HIT IN THE FACE BY A YELLOW SCHOOL BUS 211

CHAPTER 35
INDUCTION PROCESS FOR POSITIVE INPUT 219

CHAPTER 36
WHO IS TOM RAY? 227

CHAPTER 37
WHAT HAPPENED TO TOM RAY? 251

CHAPTER 38
LETTERS...I GET LETTERS 261

THE FINAL REVELATION 283

TOM RAY'S TAPES FOR SALE 284

PREFACE

The Laws of the Subconscious are now available for the first time. I often wonder why some great scientist did not step forth with this information a long time before I did. I was taught to be a non-reader, even though both of my parents were great teachers. I was average-to-poor in math and chemistry, even though my Dad was a whiz at math and was a college chemistry teacher. I failed English and logic in college, even though my Mom was an English teacher. I could never type more than 23 words a minute. I have a computer and I barely know how to turn it on. I have been fired from almost every job I have ever had. Why, then, am I writing this book to provide information to the world? Read this book and then, you make the call!

FOREWORD

When I refer to The Puzzle Factory Syndrome, I am characterizing the human Subconscious. This human Subconscious, which is designed to protect us, can take 20 to 30 year-old, untrue, totally illogical information, add new information to the old, divide that with three different smells, two sounds and three reasonable situations, and cause you to do things that are not good for you. It can also have you do things that could very well get you killed!

In other words, the Subconscious will do what it thinks is right, in order to protect you, even though you may get hurt in the process. The human Subconscious Mind controls every function of the body. It is so very easy to change old habits, to speed the healing process, and to modify any body function for success, health, and happiness.

In The Puzzle Factory Syndrome, I have explained, in simple and understandable terms, how to use the Laws of the Subconscious to overrule the Subconscious, so that you become Successful, Healthy, and Happy Today!

Learn and use these laws and experience favorable changes in your life, NOW!

If you are already successful, healthy, and happy, you had better read this book. It will teach you to stay that way.

DEDICATION

This book is dedicated to my wife, Judy. Had it not been for her many talents, help and perseverance, this book would not be in print. If you meet her, give her a pat on the back. She truly deserves every bit of recognition she gets.

DISCLAIMER

Before you start reading this book, understand that when people came to me to be hypnotized, they were not hypnotized. They simply attained a state of perfect concentration and relaxation, and in that condition, they became very suggestible.

This book is nothing more than my thoughts and words about how to help make your life better, by using the Laws of the Subconscious. I do not write drug prescriptions. I am not a medical doctor. If you need medical attention, call your medical doctor, now!

Write to me and tell me of your successes after reading this book. Who knows? Maybe your stories will help someone else, in my next book!

INTRODUCTION

This book was conceived back in the early days of the 1980's. As my life had progressed and as I took on another job, this being about my fiftieth, I knew that someday I would no longer be a professional hypnotist. I dealt with some unusual situations and stories as a professional hypnotist, and realized that it might help other people to hear these stories.

I began to write short stories about the people that came into my office and their situations. I changed their stories in certain ways, so as not to violate any confidences, while maintaining creditability to the experience.

As I continued to help people from all walks of life, it became apparent to me that their situations were not important to the solution of their problems. What became important was the way in which my clients (not my patients) had arrived at their seemingly unsolvable dilemmas. Even more importantly, I figured out how to easily correct the so-called unsolvable situations.

As I worked and analyzed what was happening in my office at the South Texas Medical Center, the answers became so very simple. After 10 years of being a professional hypnotist and writing and rewriting my Laws of the Subconscious, here we are, in a new millennium.

This book is now in your hands. You can put it back on the shelf and continue your life as it has been for years, or you can purchase it, take it home and enjoy reading it. After reading this book, you will probably wonder why it took so long for someone to step forward with the real story about what your mind will do to you, as well as what your mind can do for you.

Success, health and happiness are simple to achieve today. Even you can do it. Read on, my friend, this is your lucky day!

CHAPTER 1

TOM RAY'S LAWS OF THE SUBCONSCIOUS

Here it is! Finally, you have your hands on a set of laws that can really improve your life. If you have been seeking answers to all your problems and looking for ways to achieve whatever your heart desires, you need look no further.

After reading this book, you will be able to deal with any situation. You will be in total control of your life, the way you have always wanted it to be. When you have mastered the school of thought contained in this book, you will then be free of all your past unpleasant experiences. You will be free to determine your own destiny. When you do as I advise, you will be a healthy, happy, successful human being. Everything that I am going to tell you will be proven over and over again to be 100% correct. To start you on the way to your new life, let us first consider your beginning.

While you were growing up, there were many people who advised and counseled you. Each one gave you information that he or she believed would benefit you by helping to shape your values and ideas. This information was given to you in sincere, good faith. Each of the people who told you things did so, because he thought the advice he was giving you was good advice or good knowledge, with which you might enhance your life. Even though some of the information was false, those people thought they were right in giving it to you. Many of those who instructed you were family and friends who had only your best interests at heart.

Unfortunately, a great deal of the knowledge you received at a young age may have sounded good, but in reality, was destructive and of no value to you. As you will soon understand, the key to your freedom is deeply rooted in your Subconscious Mind. Due to the information you were given when you were young, it would be fair to say that in some areas of your upbringing you were trained backwards. This book will help you make the changes you want to make in your life, for now and in the future.

Now, as an adult, you have, in most areas of your life, nice things happening, and in other areas of your life, you have some situations you don't really care for. You would not intentionally have the negative things happen in your life if you knew how to prevent them.

I am going to give you some new laws of life to live by. You can use these new laws to rid yourself of any and all negative situations. You do not have to use these laws, but as an intelligent, thinking human being, once you see the positive results these laws produce in your life, you would be foolish not to take advantage of them. These laws affect no one, but you. They serve primarily to help you govern your own life. As you use these laws, no one will know that you are using them. THESE LAWS APPLY ONLY TO THE RELATIONSHIP YOUR MIND HAS WITH YOUR BODY. After extensive research and the discarding of mounds of technical jargon, I simply call these laws, The Laws of the Subconscious.

There are laws that govern every situation. All man has to do is seek out and find the laws. For example, the law of gravity has always been present, yet it took a man's curiosity and seeking to recognize and explain this law to mankind. I am not Newton and I am not Einstein. These men developed explanations for laws that control the universe. I am Tom Ray and I will explain to you, The Laws of the Subconscious. These laws will enable you to be in complete control of your life.

The further you progress in this book, the more you will realize that you are just as capable as any person that has ever walked the face of this earth. You will realize that you have the potential to control your "universe." That great capability is in your mind. You will use your mind for your benefit and for the benefit of those you wish to help, with the understanding that the bottom line is: you only have to help yourself.

You must understand that The Laws of the Subconscious have been proven time and time again, so keep an open mind and read and understand what I have to say. These laws are fact. These laws have absolutely nothing to do with religion; nothing to do with hope; nothing to do with belief. They are facts that relate your mind to your body. I know a lot of people that have died using hope. Use your head and good common sense; take action and you will make it.

There are 12 Laws of the Subconscious. It is important to remember that the Subconscious acts as a computer and records all life experiences. It does not, however, have the ability to reason. Let me now list these laws, so that you can get a clear picture of them. Then I will discuss them.

1. You own a Conscious Mind and a Subconscious Mind. The Conscious Mind, a waking, thinking, reasoning state, controls the Subconscious Mind.

2. The Subconscious Mind controls the total body function.

3. If you do not consciously control the Subconscious Mind, it will control you.

4. The tools you use to control the Subconscious Mind consist of your thoughts, your words, and the way in which you perceive things.

5. Whatever you put into your Subconscious Mind, be it positive or negative, will have a like effect on your body.

6. The Subconscious Mind records every experience you have.

7. The Subconscious Mind computes every experience to be either positive or negative.

8. The Subconscious Mind understands only *yes* or *no*.

9. Feelings are a choice.

10. The Subconscious Mind assigns a meaning to each of the words that you use and to each thought that you have.

11. The Subconscious Mind can only function in the time frame: NOW.

12. You do your own thinking; you choose your own thoughts.

Now that you have seen The Laws of the Subconscious in print, let me explain them, one by one.

First Law: "You own a Conscious Mind and a Subconscious Mind. The Conscious Mind, a waking, thinking, reasoning state, controls the so-called Subconscious Mind."

The word "Subconscious" is used for the lack of a better word. When we say "Subconscious," we mean that it is the mind beneath the Conscious. It takes its orders directly from the Conscious. Therefore, the Conscious Mind controls and influences the Subconscious Mind.

Second Law: "The Subconscious Mind controls the total body function."

This is a simple statement of fact. Here we begin to see the basic pattern for life and survival. The Conscious Mind controls the Subconscious Mind, and the Subconscious Mind controls the body function.

Third Law: "If you do not consciously control the Subconscious Mind, the Subconscious Mind will control you."

The information that the Subconscious uses to control you is that information stored in your Memory Bank. As I said earlier, much of that information is untrue. As a result, the Subconscious may lead you down the wrong path. To clarify this law, let me say that one of the functions of the Subconscious Mind is to record everything in your life's experience. This record is called your Memory Bank.

Another function of the Subconscious Mind is to release information to your Conscious Mind.

If the information in your Memory Bank is all positive, then all Conscious Mind functions and, therefore, all body functions will be positive.

It then follows that, if your Memory Bank holds negative information, your Conscious Mind and body functions can draw on this information to create negative situations in your life. This allows your Subconscious Mind to control you.

You must consciously control your Subconscious Mind by choosing only positive information to be placed in your Memory Bank.

Fourth Law: "The tools you use to control the Subconscious Mind consist of your thoughts, your words, and the way in which you perceive things."

In other words, the way you think, what you say, and your process of reasoning in your Conscious Mind will control your Subconscious Mind. With the use of only positive thoughts, words, and perceptions, you will have positive results. If you have only positive or good input, then everything you draw from your Subconscious Mind will be positive or good.

Fifth Law: "Whatever you put into your Subconscious Mind, be it positive or negative, will have a like effect on your body."

This law is an especially important one, as it is a kind of summary of the first four Laws. You own a Subconscious Mind. It belongs only to you. And because you own one, you should know how it works.

We have established that the Subconscious Mind operates like a computer and what you put into the computer, you will get out.

To illustrate this fact, let's compare your Subconscious Mind and the effect it has on your body, to a piggy bank that has the ability to have feelings. If you put a dollar in the piggy bank, it will smile. The smile is a signal that the bank feels good and is happy with the dollar. However, put a counterfeit dollar in the bank, and it will frown, as a signal that it feels bad and is unhappy with the counterfeit dollar.

So, it makes no difference what money you put in the bank, it will always show feelings related to what is put inside it. Also, whatever is put into the piggy bank will, at some time, be given back to you.

This is what occurs in the relationship between your Subconscious Mind and your body. Whatever you put into your Subconscious Mind, be it positive or negative, will have a like effect on your body. Exactly what you put into your Subconscious Mind will cause your body to react accordingly. These feelings will be expressed by your feeling either good or bad.

Sixth Law: "The Subconscious Mind records every experience you have."

It records everything you hear, see, touch, smell, and every feeling you have experienced in your entire life. The Subconscious Mind also records the time and conditions under which your feelings were experienced.

Seventh Law: "The Subconscious Mind computes every experience to be either positive or negative."

The Conscious Mind acts as a "Traffic Cop" by directing each experience to go to the positive side of the computer or the negative side of the computer, depending on existing information already recorded on either side. The computer is, of course, your Subconscious Mind.

Eighth Law: "When commanding the Subconscious Mind, it will only act on *yes* or *no*."
It doesn't understand *maybe*; *I hope so*; or *I will try*. It only understands *yes* and *no*. When dealing with your Subconscious Mind, you must be totally clear. There can be no vagueness in your commands to it.

Ninth Law: "Feelings are a choice."
If you let the Subconscious rule your life, your feelings will be given to you automatically, based on the existing information stored in your Memory Bank. When you were a child, you were taught that certain things would make you mad, upset, nervous, depressed, etc. and because your Subconscious does what it is told, you reacted accordingly.

The feelings your Subconscious Mind gives you may be uncomfortable feelings. If you do get uncomfortable feelings, it is because you have, in the past, given your Subconscious Mind negative thoughts or negative information.

Now, since you can consciously choose the types of "dollars" or the types of thoughts that go into your Memory Bank, or your Subconscious Mind, why not choose only good thoughts, make positive statements and see the good side of all situations, so that you will always have good feelings?

Protect yourself, but see the good in all things. It's purely a word game between you and your Subconscious. For example, no one can make you mad. If you choose to get mad, then that feeling is based on previous teaching and information that has been deposited in your Subconscious Mind. You do not have to react physiologically the way people tell you to react. Why should you get mad, upset, nervous, sick, etc.?

Tenth Law: "The Subconscious Mind assigns a meaning to each of the words that you use and to each thought that you have."

At this point, we can say that your words and your thoughts become commands to the Subconscious Mind when they are placed in the right format. When you use the words, *I, me, myself, we, ours,* or any other word which designates yourself, and you use it with a firm *yes* or *no,* it becomes a direct command to the Subconscious.

It follows, then, that it would be foolish to command yourself to be mad, upset, depressed, sick, frustrated, or unhappy. To go back to the feeling of being mad, ask yourself exactly what the meaning of the word "mad" is. The word itself, was first associated with rabies and meant "foaming at the mouth; sick or dying."

Why would you consciously choose to experience or feel any of those conditions? The Subconscious Mind, because it is designed to take care of you, will give you whatever you command. If you command a "mad" feeling, the Subconscious understands "mad" and will produce the commanded response.

Eleventh Law: "The Subconscious Mind can only function in the time frame, NOW."

The Subconscious Mind does not understand time, so we must establish a time in which the Subconscious can operate. There must be a time for you to do all the wonderful things you are going to do for yourself, so we will command a time for the Subconscious.

Let us draw an imaginary line on the ground and call that line the time frame, NOW. One side of the line will be called the PAST and the other side of the line will be called the FUTURE. In reality, the time element, PAST does not exist, because the past has already gone. You can produce pictures of the past, things made in the past, or talk about the past, but the PAST does not exist, anymore.

How about the FUTURE? It does not exist either. It has simply not arrived yet. The only thing that we can be absolutely sure of is the present, or the NOW.

If the NOW is the only time that you live in, it would be foolish to worry about yesterday or what happened yesterday; or to worry about tomorrow or what might happen tomorrow. What you must be concerned about is only the NOW. Remember, the Subconscious only understands NOW.

If you try to make your Subconscious deal with the PAST or the FUTURE, you will get a "feel-bad." Planning is O.K. Worry is thinking about the negatives that may happen in the FUTURE. You don't know anything about the FUTURE. No one does. So, deal only in the NOW.

Twelfth Law: "You do your own thinking; you choose your own thoughts."

We also know now that you choose your own feelings. Because of this fact, why not choose only good feelings, regardless of what other people do or say. By choosing only good feelings, you no longer have problems.

You are to eliminate the word "problem" from your vocabulary and use the word, "situations." You were trained that problems have to be solved, and if you don't solve them, you will have a "feel-bad." Whereas, situations can be either dealt with, set aside, or forgotten. With your new knowledge of how to program your Subconscious Mind, you can now deal with every situation in a positive manner and therefore, you have no problem.

Those are the 12 Laws of the Subconscious Mind. You and I have a little situation, now. You have been reading what I have to say and because you were taught to be analytical, to question, to doubt, to wonder, to figure and to argue, you have been doing just that.

It is good that you were taught to question, doubt, wonder, figure, and argue, but when you are controlling the Subconscious, there is no room for these doubts. The Subconscious is simply going to respond as you command. If you question yourself; if you doubt yourself; if you argue with yourself; you will be placing yourself back into a negative situation.

In order to overcome the negative conditioning that was performed on you as you were growing up, you must now be in charge of your own conditioning. It is now time for you to control your life and not allow others to control you. They may not control you to your satisfaction. You know what you like and what you dislike. Why not make yourself the person you want to be NOW?

Because of the First Law: "You consciously control the Subconscious," it is now time to start your reconditioning process. What happens in the reconditioning process? You take charge of the Subconscious and tell it how things are to be. This process requires conscious thought on your part.

Take a comfortable position, either in an easy chair or

on the bed. Make sure that the area is quiet. The purpose of this is to do away with all outside distractions. You are to use a procedure that I will give you later, for relaxing the body. As time goes on, you will realize you can command the Subconscious in any situation, even while standing in the middle of a noisy crowd, walking down the street, or running from a wild animal.

The purpose of relaxing the body is to minimize outside distractions and increase concentration. When the body is perfectly relaxed, the Subconscious seems to act on the commands with unbelievable speed! And you CAN be relaxed while running from that wild animal! If you think to yourself, "I cannot relax," then this thought becomes a command and you will not relax.

Understand that your thoughts are commands. You must remember the Fifth Law. The Subconscious Mind operates like a computer. This has nothing to do with what is right, or what is wrong, or religion, or anything else. This process is purely a mechanical process. You must mechanically put the good "dollar" in the "bank" and you mechanically get a good or favorable response. Your body is like a machine, and the performance you get will depend on how you treat it.

I had a preacher in my office one day, and he said that when he told himself he was relaxed, he felt like he was lying to himself. In his mind, he would argue, "But I am not relaxed." When he put in two conflicting statements: "I am relaxed" and "I am not relaxed," he received an uncomfortable feeling and then identified it to mean that he was lying to himself, because of the two thoughts being in direct conflict. The Subconscious cannot understand *yes* and *no* in the same thought. So make up your mind to say, "I am relaxed" and simply leave it at that!

To prove to yourself that what I say to you is fact, set this book aside and close your eyes. Repeat to yourself the following: Use your first name or the name you call yourself, followed by the word, "relax." Do this repeatedly, over and over for about one minute, then judge for yourself. Example: "Tom, relax; Tom, relax; Tom, relax; Tom, relax; Tom, relax" and so on, for about one full minute. It is amazing! As I sit here and type these words, I can feel my body relax even more! Be sure to pick up this book again and continue reading. There is more to come!

The first thing you must say to the Subconscious is that you are a changed person, NOW. You are no longer the person you used to be. You have simply changed the way that you think, speak, and perceive things. Because of the NOW, you must say that you are NOW changed. It would be a waste of your time to say, "I am trying to change," or "I would like to change." Remember, the Subconscious only understands the NOW time period.

Now that you are changed, what kind of a person are you NOW? You will only use positive commands, like the following:

*I am a perfectly relaxed person.

*I am a perfectly healthy person. *(Sick or not, you must say, "I am a perfectly healthy person and getting better every day." This leaves no room for doubt.)*

*I am in charge of my Subconscious, and it gives me exactly what I command.

*I choose my own feelings and I choose only good feelings.

*I am a very confident person.

*I am always honest.

*I see the good side of all situations.

*I do what I want to do; I do not do what I do not want to do. *(This is within the confines of the law. If you don't like the law, join a group, go to the polls and vote in new laws that you like.)*

*Nothing bothers me.

*I am a positive person.

*I am unconcerned about the thoughts of other persons, because I cannot see inside their minds. *(I care for and love others, but I keep ME healthy first, so I can help those I love.)*

*What others say or do to me does not bother me, because they may not understand their own feelings and actions.

*I protect myself first, so that I can stay healthy, in order to protect those I care for.

*Those things that happened in the past that were uncomfortable mean nothing now, because the past does not exist.

*I plan for the future, but I am happy with myself, NOW!

I am sure that the above statements sound a little strange to you. However, you must say or think to yourself the good information, in order to get out good feelings and results.

Every statement or command that you make to yourself MUST be given in the present tense. Make every statement as though it were fact, NOW. This is the key to success. The Subconscious will simply act to make it true.

What do you think a "goal" is? It is a constant thought of something that you wish to attain. Now you know why goals are often met. People keep their goals ever present in their minds. What is "thought"? It is a command to the Subconscious.

Life is very simple and exciting now, because you simply make it that way. You know now that you make your own luck. You make your own excitement. You make your own health. Stay in touch with your doctor, but be responsible for your own health. YOU are in charge now. Do what YOU want to do. Be what YOU want to be. It's up to YOU!

After reading this book, go back and read this chapter three or four times, until you know the information perfectly. Many people will read a "how-to" book and simply not use what they have read. Why read it and agree with it and not use it? You are an intelligent person. I am sure you will use what you read in this book!

If you would like to hear my voice give you the favorable commands, there is a list of my audiocassette tapes and order form at the end of this book.

CHAPTER 2

MEET THE WAGNERS

(THE WAGNERS ARE NOT A REAL FAMILY. *I made up this family to show you, the reader, that by using the Laws of the Subconscious, the Wagners were able to solve the many everyday problems that prevented them from being Successful, Healthy, and Happy. If you are already Successful, Healthy, and Happy, congratulations! Keep on reading, because this book will help keep you that way.*)

Mr. and Mrs. Wagner have just paid their $500.00 to my receptionist so that they can each spend four hours with me, Tom Ray, the world's greatest professional hypnotist. They have decided to trade in their "feel-bads" for "feel-goods," so that they can deal with, or better yet, eliminate the many problems that they have. Fortunately, you do not have to spend $500.00 to get what you desire in this life. Just read this book and the answers are yours to use forever.

"How are you today, Mr. Wagner? Please take the green chair. Mrs. Wagner, would you please take the other chair?" I walk around to my desk, where I have an old, brown high-back office chair that leans a little to the left, because of 10 years of slow, steady rocking back and forth. If I lean too far back, the old chair has a tendency to fall backwards, so I have to prop it up against the wall for stability. My desk is an old World War II military desk that has been stripped and refinished. Off to the right of the desk sets a soft, black lounge that looks as though one would fall asleep by just lying down on it. On my back wall, I have a collection of the San Antonio Spurs' pictures. The Spurs are

San Antonio's own NBA professional basketball team. I believe I should be on the Spurs' coaching staff, right behind the assistant coaches and the trainer. I love pro basketball!

As I pick up my pipe,* light it, and open the Wagners' folder, I begin the conversation. "Well, folks, why are you here?" The reason I open with this question, even though the Wagners have answered about three pages of written questions, is to hear exactly what they say when they talk about their problems. As you will read later on in this book, what a person actually speaks and thinks has a direct effect on his own Subconscious Mind and then, directly on his body, regarding his health and his actions. Mrs. Wagner begins, "Well, Dr. Ray..."

"Please, Mrs. Wagner. I am not a doctor. Just call me Tom."

Mrs. Wagner is sitting on the edge of the chair and starts to speak again. "Well, Tom..."

Again I interrupt, "Please sit back in the chair and relax. That is one of the things that I teach athletes that are sitting on the sidelines waiting to go into the game. If they sit back and relax, they will be refreshed, and when they are called to go into the game, they will not be worn out from being too tense and tight. So, sit back and tell me how I can help you."

Mrs. Wagner begins again. "I am a real nervous person and I have been awfully depressed lately. I am under a lot of stress and strain, partly as a result of my job. Also, my husband and I haven't been getting along too well, lately. He drinks too much and he stays out too late at night. I would like to get off these Valiums that my doctor has prescribed for me and I need to lose a little weight and give

---

I have since chosen not to smoke.

up my nasty smoking habit. I am not happy, anymore. It is not like it used to be. I guess I am getting old."

"Well, have a cigarette and relax," I say. "What brand do you smoke?" Then, I open the desk drawer and pull out about twelve or thirteen partially full packs of different brands of cigarettes and dump them on the corner of the desk. After she takes a cigarette from one of the packs, I rake them off the desk back into the drawer. "You folks can thank your lucky stars that you came to see me, because I am the world's best hypnotist. Had you gone to someone else...well, that is unimportant. Let's continue. Mr. Wagner, sir, why are you here?"

"I have these terrible migraine headaches. I drink too much. And my business is going down the tubes. I am afraid to ask my wife for sex, because I am starting to get impotent. It looks as if life is passing me by. My good years are gone, forever. Also, that son and daughter of ours are about to drive us up the wall. They are both on drugs and they have become two irresponsible, worthless teenagers. Every time I buy them a new car, they just wreck it. I am about to run out of money. I am at my rope's end. You are our only hope."

"Hoping is a waste of time. Hope can get you killed. I know a lot of people that died, just sitting around hoping. It is time to correct all of this. You can be thankful you came to me. I am going to show you how to be happy, healthy, successful, and eliminate all of your problems."

Mr. and Mrs. Wagner slump back in their chairs, as though two tons of weight had been lifted from their shoulders. "I am going to ask you fine folks some questions that may sound a little obvious or strange, but there is a reason for the questions and the way they are asked. So, when I ask, just answer. If I am not talking to you personally, please keep your comments to yourself and do not try to answer for the other person. O.K.?" Then I smile politely at each of them, indicating that I mean what I say. They love it, because I have taken the lead and I sound as though I have the answers, which is why they came to me.

"Mrs. Wagner, ma'am, what type of person are you?" I ask.

"I don't know," she answers. "What do you mean?"

"Are you loud, quiet, easy-going, overbearing?"

Mr. Wagner blurts out, "She is overbearing."

Mrs. Wagner confirms, "He is right."

"Mr. Wagner, what type of person are you?" I ask.

"I have a bad temper and I am afraid I yell too much at the kids," he admits.

His wife adds, "Yes, we do not ever agree when it comes to correcting the children. He is too rough on our son, but he lets our daughter get away with anything. I am just so sick, because of the way he treats the kids, I do not know what to do."

"Mrs. Wagner, do you ever get mad?" I ask.

"Why, yes. Everybody gets mad," she says.

"I don't," I assert, "and later, I will explain why I say that. What can make you mad?"

Mrs. Wagner proclaims, "Anything can make me mad. I stay mad and upset about half the time. My husband can make me mad more than anything can. He is just not the same man I married. I've had it. I'm ready to throw in the towel. I would probably be better off dead."

"Do you ever get nervous?" I ask.

"I was born nervous," states Mrs. Wagner. "I stay that way. If I don't die from a heart attack, my ulcers will kill me."

"What can make you nervous, Mrs. Wagner," I

inquire.

"Everything. Especially my elderly mother. She is still trying to run my life. She has never liked my husband, from the day we were married, and we have been married about 25 years now."

I turn to her husband. "Mr. Wagner, sir, what can make you mad?"

Mrs. Wagner interrupts, "His temper is terrible!"

I remind her, "Please, Mrs. Wagner, I asked you not to speak unless the questions are directed to you."

"Yes, that is one of her worse traits," comments Mr. Wagner. "She is always interrupting me. I can't get in a word edgewise when I am around her. If she would quit talking, maybe I could think. What makes me mad? You are looking at it! Her!"

It is obvious that these two people love each other, but you could not tell it to hear them talk.

Mr. Wagner continues, "I guess I do lose my temper too much. If you had the type of job I have, you would lose your temper, too."

In my mind, I simply blocked that command and said, "NO." I will explain later what I am talking about: blocking verbal commands mentally, so that the command will not be carried out on me at a later date.

I ask, "What do you do for a living, Mr. Wagner?"

"I am half-owner of the Acme Mortuary and Grave-Digging Service. You know me...I am the last one to ever let you down."

He chuckles, and his wife is obviously not impressed with his humor. "But I have a partner that is stupid, and stupidity makes me madder than anything."

I ask, "Why don't you buy him out and get rid of

him?"

"I just don't have the money. The economy has been bad lately. People are not dying off as fast, and my competition has a major part of the market covered up."

He chuckles again, while saying, "No pun intended. Besides, I have to spend all my money on my wife and my two worthless kids."

"Mr. Wagner, on a scale of 1 to 10, with 1 being a chimpanzee and 10 being an Einstein, what would you consider your intelligence level to be?"

"I am about average. I would say 5 or 6," he replies.

I ask, "Mrs. Wagner, on a scale of 1 to 10, with 1 being not able to stand yourself, and 10 being in love with yourself, what do you think about yourself?"

"I haven't been feeling too good about myself, lately. I will pick about a 3."

I ask Mr. Wagner, " On a scale of 1 to 10, what is your confidence level? With 1, you have no confidence. With 10, you are the most confident person in the world."

" I used to be a very confident person, but now I would say that I am about a 4."

I ask Mrs. Wagner, "Do you have any faults?"

"Certainly. Doesn't everybody have faults?"

"I do not," I state, "and I will explain later why I have made this statement."

As Mr. and Mrs. Wagner are talking, I continue making notes. After all the questions, I lay their folders on my desk, and, with a rested look on my face, lean back in my chair. I tell them again, that they have come to the right place.

"Folks, it is very simple. I am going to tell you what the problem is. I am going to tell you how you got it, and I am going to show you how we are going to eliminate it. Then we are going to eliminate it. I ask you now to hold your questions for a while, and I am going to do the talking. So, please listen to me very carefully, because what I have to say is extremely important. Even though I may not be talking directly to you, you are to assume that I am talking to you.

Now, the problem started the day that you were born. Let's say, hypothetically, that you started your learning process the day you were born. We now know that a child does hear and feel certain things before birth. But, for practical purposes, let us say that your birthday is the day your real education started. The people that educated you...family, church, school, neighbors, friends, radio, TV, magazines; these people handed information down to you that they felt to be true. The problem is that these people knew little about the Science of the Mind and its relationship to the body. They thought they knew, but they didn't. They understood math, chemistry, physics, electricity, and many other things, but they didn't know enough about the mind and how it works in conjunction with the body.

I am going to give you a new set of laws to live by, and if you stay within these laws and do not break them, everything will go your way. I mean everything: excellent health, success, happiness...everything. You, being wise and intelligent people, would not intentionally break the laws of electricity, because you might get hurt. But, you have been breaking the Laws of the Subconscious, and it has been creating problems for you. So, I am first going to re-educate you. It is obvious that if you knew what the Laws of the Subconscious were, and how these Laws pertain to your body, you would stay within the Laws.

The first Law is the Law of Ownership. You own

something that we are going to call a "Subconscious," for lack of a better term. This Subconscious Mind runs your body. Set aside all your information about medicine for a moment. The Subconscious was here before Louis Pasteur or the study of the sciences came along.

The Subconscious is your computer. It regulates every function of your body. It regulates your heartbeat, your breathing rate, your strength, your ability to heal, your blood's ability to coagulate, your ability to sing, dance, walk, talk, think; in short, every function of the body.

You also own a Conscious Mind, and that Conscious Mind can overrule or control the Subconscious Mind. If the Subconscious rules the body, and the Conscious can rule the Subconscious, then, through the normal chain of command, the Conscious Mind can rule the body by controlling the Subconscious.

If you do not consciously control the Subconscious, it will control you. There is only one thing wrong with your Subconscious controlling you. And here it is: the only information that the Subconscious has is that information that is stored in your Memory Bank. Unfortunately, some of the information in the Memory Bank is untrue.

The people that educated you did not know the Laws of the Subconscious; therefore, they accidentally told you things that were just not true. You have been working with untrue information, and that untrue information has created problems for you.

The people that gave you all of this information simply thought they were helping you. They gave you untruths, thinking they were truths. You accepted this information and used it, and now you have problems. The majority of the information that you have received over the years has been truthful and it has created a lot of good things for you, but the untrue information has created problems for you.

I am going to tell you what is true and what is not true, as far as the mind and its relationship with the body is concerned. Both of you, being sound and intelligent people, would not command your Subconscious with lies or lousy commands, and you would not give untruths or no-good commands to yourself or your loved ones. Unfortunately, that is what you have been doing. You have been accepting the wrong kinds of commands from others and you have been using no-good commands on yourselves.

Maybe you are wondering, what is a command to the Subconscious, and how does one block commands from others? By the way, if the Subconscious is doing a good job in a particular area, leave that to the Subconscious. If your blood pressure is O.K., leave that alone. If your sweat glands work fine, leave them alone, but correct those things that are not to your satisfaction. The things that seem to be common are pain, disease, stress, depression, overweight, underweight, smoking, sexual problems, backaches, stomach aches, and the list goes on.

With the help of those that educated you, plus your not knowing the Laws of the Subconscious, you have been keeping your problems ongoing, and even making them worse. If the world would adopt these Laws of the Subconscious, we could turn all of the hospitals into resort centers for fun, and keep the emergency clinics for accidents.

If you are going to control your Subconscious, thereby controlling your body for the good things, how are you going to do it? You first need to know how the Subconscious works. For one, the Subconscious records everything that you have ever said, heard, felt, smelled, tasted, and thought. When you know how to control the Subconscious, you can simply draw that information out of your Subconscious Memory Bank. That means that you have a photographic mind, but you were not taught that. You were taught that you could forget things.

Forgetting is impossible, when you know how to control your Subconscious. It is possible not to recall a particular thing at a particular time, but it is impossible to forget. See that is just one of the many little lies we were taught. We were taught that we could forget...and that is just not true.

Besides recording and giving back information when asked for properly, how else does the Subconscious work? Let's say that the Subconscious works like a small piggybank. This bank has the ability to smile, or to have a "feel-good." It will make a favorable action or have a favorable reaction when it receives the good dollar.

The reverse happens when it receives the counterfeit dollar. The bank has a "feel-bad," which is an unfavorable action or an unfavorable reaction. What you folks have been doing is, you have been putting the wrong type of dollar in your banks. You have also allowed others to put in the wrong kind of dollar for you.

The dollar to the bank is actually like commands to your Subconscious Mind that will be carried out without question. In other words, you have been accidentally commanding your Subconscious with the wrong kind of commands, and you have accidentally received from others the wrong kind of commands to your Subconscious. Then, when you acted out the commands or had the "feel-bads," you may have wondered why you felt bad or did the things you did.

The Subconscious Mind is totally illogical. It makes no difference what type of command it receives, be it illogical or be it untrue. It simply takes the command and acts it out. If it is the wrong type of command, you will get the wrong or unfavorable response.

This procedure requires no belief or acceptance. The bank takes the dollar or command and it is recorded. It is automatically received and then acted upon. So, I do not necessarily ask you to believe me or to understand me. Simply do as I say.

As I said, the Subconscious can be commanded or triggered through any of the senses. If you hear a train whistle, you think of a train and then you may concern yourself with your safety, depending on your relationship to the train tracks. If you smell smoke, you will have a thought process that will involve several things.

Even though you will continue to rely on your senses for information sources, you are primarily going to use word patterns and thought patterns to manipulate your Subconscious, thereby taking control of your own health and success.

When I say "word patterns," I mean "word placement." You can take ten particular words and put them in a sentence and it will mean one thing. Then, if you rearrange the same ten words, you may have a different meaning. There is no telling how many different meanings you could get from ten particular words. If word placement and thought placement can constitute a command, then what type of word placement and what type of thought placement are actually commands to the Subconscious?

When you use a word that indicates YOU, such as, *your name, I, me, myself,* obviously you are talking about yourself. If you use the words, *you, he, she, them, they,* you are directing your command toward someone else. If you use or hear the words, *we, us, our,* you are included in the command automatically.

At this time, it is necessary to explain to you that the Subconscious only understands *yes* or *no*, when action is required. In other words, the Subconscious can only handle one end of the spectrum or the other. It can only work off of an absolute *yes* or *no*. Anything in between will not be acted upon.

This makes it so simple. Anything other than a *yes* or *no* constitutes no command, and you will not get the desired response. So, the command to the Subconscious becomes *I:yes* or *I:no*. A form of *I:yes* and *I:no* is: *I am* or *I am not*; *I do* or *I do not*; *I have* or *I have not*. These are absolutes and will get you the desired response. Like I said, the Subconscious cannot handle anything in between, such as, *I need to; I would like to; I want to; I hope so; I will try.*

You can command the Subconscious with thought. The way you see the situation can create a "feel-good" or a "feel-bad." Let's say that you came upon a train wreck where there were 500 casualties and 500 survivors. The good side of the situation is that here are 500 that survived. The other side is that there were 500 that were lost because of faulty tracks. You can do nothing about the 500 that have died. They are dead. That cannot be changed. You do not like what you see, but you would be wasting your time with a "feel-bad." If you had a "feel-bad," how could you stay healthy and stable enough to help those who may need your help? If your "feel-bad" is too great, you might wind up in the hospital with depression and you would be no good to yourself or to anyone else.

"Feel-bads" are a waste of time. The only way you can have a "feel-bad" is to create it yourself. By programming myself now, if I lose a loved one, in the future, I will survive with a minimum of "feel-bads." When I die, I hope that all my friends and family will get together and have a big party and remember the good times they had with ol' Tom Ray. If they sit around and cry, they will just waste their time. Their "feel-bads" won't do me a bit of good and it will do them a lot of harm. There are countries on this old earth of ours where it is the law that you must mourn for at least two years. Kind of ridiculous, don't you think? Lay the dead to rest gracefully, and continue living.

Let's see, Mr. and Mrs. Wagner, what commands you have been accepting from others. But first, let me explain that you were not trained to listen to individual words. You were trained to listen to the sentence or the phrase, and then, to draw your conclusion or to make your assumption.

Your Subconscious records each and every word. Where there is an absolute *yes* or *no*, it will act upon those words. So you had better be careful before you open your mouth and say, *I:yes* or *I:no*. If you use *maybe*, this is nothing more than *yes* and *no* at the same time.

If you use any form of *yes* and *no* at the same time, you will create conflict for the Subconscious. It will then automatically send you a small "feel-bad" in order to warn you to get off the *yes* and *no* and to get on with *yes* or *no*.

For example: Let us say that we were planning to go fishing, Mr. Wagner. I ask you to buy the boat, bait, gear, and fishing licenses, and to call me Friday night, so I can tell you where we are going to fish. You call Friday night and ask, "Tom, are we going to go fishing?" and I say to you, "*yes* and *no*."

You say, "Hey, I bought all this equipment and you told me that we were going to go fishing. Are we going to go or not? Tell me *yes* or *no!*"

I say, "Mr. Wagner, *yes* and *no*."

"Say, Tom Ray, are we going? Give me a *yes* or a *no*. Yes and *no* just doesn't get it. Make up your mind. *Yes* or *no!*"

That uncomfortable feeling that Mr. Wagner would begin to experience is nothing more than the Subconscious sending him a message that something is not going right or that he is perceiving this situation to be no-good. So, we can say, at this point, that the way you perceive a situation will determine your "feel-good" or "feel-bad."

I must explain to you at this time, that there are two sides to every situation: a good side and the other side. Notice, I did not say the bad side. If you conclude that a situation has a bad side, you get the "feel-bad." The whole idea is to see the good side for the "feel-good" and see the other side for information and for your protection.

To show you how picky the Subconscious is, and to explain that the Subconscious reacts to words individually, I am going to ask you three questions. You will answer the first two questions incorrectly and you will answer the last one right. Your Subconscious will respond properly on all three, but you will give me a different answer than your Subconscious gives on the first two. On the third question, you will give me the same answer that your Subconscious gives.

Mr. Wagner, would you tell me the color of that couch

in the corner?"

"It is black."

"Wrong. You are not listening to the question. Mrs. Wagner, will you tell me the color of your dress?"

"My dress is blue."

"Wrong again. You people are just not listening to the question. Mr. Wagner, would you sign over to me all of your assets; give me those two fine kids of yours; you leave town and send me 90% of everything you make; don't argue; don't complain; don't call the law; and be happy with your decision?"

"No!"

"Correct. I just asked you a *yes* or *no* question. On the first two questions, I did not ask you for the color. I asked if you would tell me the color. I asked for a simple *yes* or *no*.

Let's see what you folks have been saying to yourselves. Let's see what your illogical Subconscious Minds have been giving you back, in the form of feelings and actions. When you first came into my office, about forty-five minutes ago, I asked what I could do for you. That's when the garbage started to flow from your mouths and your minds. The commands that you have given yourselves in the past were simply reinforced by what you have said here in my office today. Let's see exactly what you said, and let's see what the Subconscious is going to do for you, in the way of a feeling or an action or a physiological reaction.

Understand that you thought you were just stating the problems, but actually, you were reinforcing the symptoms. Example: Mrs. Wagner said, "I am a real nervous person." Remember that anything after, *"I am"* will simply be acted out with the exact feelings and responses. The Subconscious simply takes the command and makes you more nervous. There may have been times that you were nervous and did nothing about it, and maybe did not understand why you were nervous. Then, there may have been another time that you were nervous and you concluded that, "I am a nervous person." The Subconscious simply says, "O.K." It makes no difference to the Subconscious what you say; the Subconscious takes it and responds accordingly.

Let's see what other negative commands you have given yourselves. I will now just simply state them. Listen to the accidental, ridiculous statements that you have commanded yourself.

I am a real nervous person.

I have been awfully depressed lately.

I am under a lot of stress and strain.

Paul and I haven't been getting along too well lately.

He drinks too much. (That is simply a command to your husband to drink too much. If you say, "You drink too much," the Subconscious responds, "O.K., let's drink too much.")

I would like to get off these Valiums. (Remember, *I would like to*, is not conclusive enough to get any action; so your words were wasted.)

I would like to lose a little weight. (The same thing applies, as in the previous statement; no command: no support from the Subconscious.)

I would like to give up my nasty smoking habit. (Let's take a good look at that statement. *I would like to give up* is not a command. *My nasty smoking habit*: *my* indicates a command; *nasty*, we have been taught, is no-good; *habit* is something that you do without thinking. Therefore, the Subconscious says, "Smoking is something nasty we do without thinking."

Based on the above command, the Subconscious is going to have you continue something that you get a "feel-bad" from, that you have simply allowed yourself to do without thinking. Plus, you are doing something and then complaining about your decision. That is a *yes* and *no* at the same time. When you do this, you are going to get the "feel-bad" as a message from the Subconscious to go with *yes* or *no*. Smoke and like it, or not smoke and like it. It is foolish to smoke and then complain. Remember, we were born knowing nothing. We were taught to think and act this way, but it was not done on purpose. Those who did it thought they were helping us.

Let's continue.

I am not happy anymore. (Subconscious says, "Have a "feel-bad.")

I guess I am getting old. (Subconscious says, "Feel and act old.")

I have these terrible migraine headaches. (Have is ownership. He owns headaches. The Subconscious says, "Head, hurt!")

I drink too much and my business is going down the tubes. (The Subconscious says, "Let's have another drink, and go broke, and have a "feel-bad.")

I am afraid to ask my wife for sex. (Your Subconscious doesn't like fear, so you simply do not ask or make any overtures that may lead to sex.)

I am starting to get impotent. (The Subconscious says "O.K." and under these conditions, you cannot perform. You do not have to ask for sex and experience fear, plus have a "feel-bad.")

Life is passing me by. (Your Subconscious says, "O.K.,

you lose. It's time to hang it up. By the way, have a "feel-bad.")

Our children have become two irresponsible and worthless teenagers. (If you have ever said this to your kids, *have become* is an absolute, and it, therefore, is a command. If your kids do not say NO to that command, they simply act out the command. Based on what you have said, they are presently acting out your commands. It is time to get tough and to get positive with your kids. You must understand, it is not entirely your fault your children are the way they are. It is a result of everything that they are exposed to in this world today. Just look around you. So, it is your job to teach them to think and speak properly.)

Every time I buy them a new car, they wreck it. (If you have ever told them this, their Subconscious Minds simply say, "New car. Let's wreck it. Daddy will buy us a new one.")

You are our only hope. (If that were the case and I turned you away, you would be up that famous creek without a paddle!)

The next Law that I am going to talk about is the *Law of Feelings*. Remember the piggy bank on the desk. This bank cannot have a "feel-good" or a "feel-bad" until you command it to do so. Therefore, we will say that feelings are a simple choice! They did not tell you this. They thought feelings were automatic. They told you this would make you mad; that would make you nervous; this would make you happy or sad, etc. Well, that is just not true.

Paul, let's you and I go back to the first day of the first grade and see where some of this erroneous information may have come from. Our parents told us to listen to our teachers, because they were right and correct and they would teach us the truth. Here is the scene: The teacher sees you and me at the back of the room talking to Charlie. She says,

"Tom, you and Paul are messing around with Charlie, and you know Charlie. He is going to get your new, yellow pencils and he is going to break them." (See, she knows Charlie has a thing for new, yellow pencils. He gets one and immediately, he breaks it. That is why she has him at the back of the room by himself.) She continues, "He is going to break your new, yellow pencils, (Here comes the command!) and you are going to get mad!" (*You are* is an absolute.)

If you get out your dictionary, you might read that "mad" means "screaming, yelling, ranting, raving, foaming at the mouth, sick and dying." "Mad" is not a good physiological place to be. "Mad" is simply body breakdown. She has told us that we were going to have physiological body breakdown when Charlie broke our pencils. I am here to tell you that I do not have to. Why can't we stay calm and relaxed as we forget it and get another pencil? Why do we have to have body breakdown? There is no connection between that broken pencil and my body.

Let's substitute some words and take another look at what the teacher told us to do. "Mad" is body breakdown . Body breakdown happens when you hit yourself on the thumb with the hammer. The teacher says, "Paul, you and Tom are messing around with Charlie and he is going to break your pencils, and when he does, you are going to pick up that hammer and hit yourself on the thumb." You tell me, Mr. and Mrs. Wagner, does that sound logical? The teacher would not make it as a teacher, if the administration heard her make a statement like that.

Let's see what you have been telling your Subconscious to do to you. Mrs. Wagner, I asked you if you ever got mad and you simply said, "Yes." I asked you, "What can make you mad?" and you told me an untruth because you did not know the Laws of the Subconscious. You said, "Anything can make me mad." I am here to tell you that are just not true. But, if you tell your illogical Subconscious that any THING can make you mad, you are in for a lot of "feel-bads."

My husband can make me mad. Mrs. Wagner, that is just not so. He may do things you do not care for, but he cannot make you mad. You make yourself mad. Your Subconscious sent you "mad" based on old commands, such as, "Your husband will do things and he will make you mad." At the time of the command, you did not say NO to block the command. So, as time went by, your husband would do things you did not like and your Subconscious sent you the "mad." By consciously overruling your Subconscious, you can consciously choose to be happy and relaxed, while you are correcting the situation or accepting the situation.

I am going to show you, Mrs. Wagner, how to place the words to Mr. Wagner, and you will have him eating out of your hand. The same goes for you, Mr. Wagner. You can have her eating out of your hand. (Read the chapter on the bear and the cookie.) I asked you, Mrs. Wagner, "Do you ever get nervous?" You stated, "I was born nervous." That is a lie, but you have been told that if you were born a particular way, that is the way it is to be; therefore, no change can take place. Buffalo cookies! You said everything makes you nervous. That is just not true. Nothing can make you nervous. YOU make you nervous. Again, if you say that everything can make you nervous, based on the way the Subconscious responds to the command, you are in for a lot of nervous "feel-bads."

It appears to me that you folks have accidentally been

promoting disaster every time you open your mouths. I know that you fine folks love each other. Remember when they told us we would grow up and fall in love. I would like to know how a person "falls" in love. Love is nothing more than a choice. Feelings are a choice and love is a feeling. They told us that we would meet a nice person who would make us happy. No one can make me happy. I have to choose to be happy to actually experience it.

By the way, you cannot make anybody happy. The whole idea is to meet a person that is already happy. How many poor suckers do you know out there trying to make someone happy or waiting for someone to come along to make them happy? It is just not going to happen. Obviously, there are things about a person that you like or do not like, but that person cannot make you happy. Being happy is strictly up to you. Now, remove the monkey that has been on your back. Be a happy person by choice. That is the only way it is going to happen!"

NOTES

CHAPTER 3
THE WAGNERS DID IT

Now that you know that feelings are a choice...if you are unhappy with your job, house, wife, husband, kids, parents, financial position, geographic location, being overprotected, or lonely, you have been wasting your time. You are in total control of your actions and feelings. Do something that will cause a change that is better to your liking.

The first thing that you must do is to tell yourself that you are happy, regardless of what happens, or regardless of the conditions. Then, you must start looking for the good side of each and every situation. If you do not like a particular situation and would like to change it, change it if you can, and if you cannot, then see the good in it and protect yourself from the bad. If you are prohibited by the law, stay within the law or help change the law. You, and only you, are the master of your destiny.

You have the ability to think; the only way you can get change is to create it. If you are stuck in a job you do not like, change. You will not starve to death. I would recommend that you find the new job before you give up the old, but you must do what you think is right for you. If you are stuck in a relationship that you do not like, give it your best shot at making it work and if it does not work, get out. You will not be alone forever. You would be surprised at how many people out there would enjoy your company.

"Now, Mr. Wagner, let's see what you commanded yourself when I asked you what your intelligence level was. You said you were a 5 or a 6. Your Subconscious takes that command and makes you act like a 5 or a 6. Your mind and Einstein's mind work exactly the same. They record information and they give back information. The only difference is the type of information recorded and the way that information is given back. So, you must command yourself to be a genius to get more favorable results. If you tell your neighbor you are a genius, he will probably have you locked up, because he does not understand the *Laws of the Subconscious*. I do not mind telling my neighbor what I think. He was not trained to think; he was trained to respond. If he does not respond favorably to a particular scene, and I want him to respond a particular way, I set another scene and wait for the response. I did not manipulate my neighbor; he became manipulated by his own previous conditioning. And I am not responsible for his previous conditioning.

One time, I was being interviewed on a radio talk show and I told the commentator that I was the world's best hypnotist. For about the next three months, there were people coming into my office saying that they heard me on the radio and that the commentator said I was the world's greatest hypnotist! The commentator did not say that. I said that. I explained to my client why I had said it. Mr. Wagner, when you called, if I had said that I did not know if I could help you or not, but bring cash first, would you have come anywhere near my office? I do not think so.

Let's see what Mrs. Wagner said to herself when I asked how she felt about herself, on a scale from 1 to 10. She said, "I haven't been feeling too good about myself lately." Whenever you attack Self, Self is going to send you a "feel-bad." Now, who do you think goes with you everywhere you go? Self. Who do you think you eat with, party with, sleep with, and bathe with? Self. You had better like Self a lot. But, remember, they taught you that you were not supposed to like Self. I do not think Jesus ever said to a person to only like himself a 5 or a 6. I do not think he ever said you should feel guilty or feel bad. He said, in effect, "Whatever you did that was not good, forget it and just do not do it again." It was one of those later churches that tried to manipulate you with false beliefs. Unfortunately, today, some religions are used to control the masses and are not designed for the welfare of the individual.

Mr. Wagner said, when I asked him what his confidence level was, "I used to be a very confident person, but now (There is that word, *now*, so everything after the word, *now*, is a command, if it is absolute.) I would say that I am a 4." No wonder your business is going down the tubes. Who wants to do business with a 4, when they can purchase from a 10! No wonder your wife talks all the time and tells you how to run your life. A 4 doesn't cut it, Mr. Wagner. How about your choosing to be a 10 in the confidence department?

I asked Mrs. Wagner if she had any faults. She said, "Doesn't everybody?" Remember, I said that I do not. When she used the word, *everybody*, that included me. If I had not blocked that command, I would be allowing my Subconscious to be told that I have faults. I simply do not tell myself that I have faults. If I do something that does not turn out right, I just do not do it again, but I do not go around criticizing myself.

By the way, the word, "perfect" is a misused word without meaning. You cannot find anything in this world that is perfect. Instead of my going around telling myself that I have faults or that I feel guilty, or that I am sorry, I say that

I am a good person and getting better every day. That way, I will get the "feel-good" from the Subconscious and that is the whole idea. When you have the "feel-goods," you can be of benefit to yourself and to those around you, if you so choose.

It is kind of like the young boy that comes to school and says, "I am a good person. I live in a nice neighborhood; I have a good dog; and I am very intelligent." The teacher would probably think he was a braggart. But if the child came in and said, "I am not too smart; I have an average mutt for a dog; and I do not like where I live," the teacher would take him under her wing like a lost chick. You tell me what is backwards. In their own way of trying to help us, people really mislead us. Of course, it is not their fault. They do not know the *Laws of the Subconscious*.

It is now time for you fine folks to change. How are you going to do it? Listen to me very carefully. Remember that the Subconscious is totally illogical. It will do as you command. Words and thoughts command the Subconscious. I will provide the words and you provide the thinking. Remember again, the Subconscious is not logical. So, here are the words.

As I hold this piece of paper, it represents the last page of "feel-bads" in your Book of Life. It represents the last personal problem; the last financial problem; the last health problem; the last job problem; the last problem of any kind that you will ever have. I turn the page and what do I see? I see a very happy person. A person that has chosen to be happy. I see a person that is calm and relaxed, regardless of what has happened or what will happen. I see a person that is a genius; that can think and not just react, unless the reaction is for good purposes. I see a person that no longer is sick or has pain. I see a person that no longer has problems; a person that only has situations. You are no longer to use the word "problem." With a problem, you only have two options: either you win or you lose. With a situation, you have a thousand options. I see a person that no longer talks, or thinks of himself as being sick, depressed, sad, upset, nervous, or having any other negative symptoms. The page is now turned. You are now changed!"

Mr. Wagner says, "Oh, my goodness, we came in here and gave this clown $500.00 and he turns the page and tell us that we are changed!"

"I believe I know what you are thinking, Mr. Wagner. You were born into a society that taught you to want to know why things happen. So, I am going to tell you why you are changed. But, first of all, I am going to ask you four questions. Mr. Wagner, who actually does your thinking?"

"She likes to, most of the time," as he turns toward his wife.

"No, that is not true. Who actually does your mechanical thinking? You do. No one else can. It is virtually impossible for someone else to do your thinking."

"Yes, you are right. I do my own thinking."

"Mrs. Wagner, who chooses your thoughts? You do, correct? I could ask you to think about this fountain pen and you could choose to think about the typewriter and I would never know the difference, correct?"

"Yes, you are correct. I choose my own thoughts."

"Mr. Wagner, under this new Law, who chooses your feelings?"

"I do."

"Then, if that is the case, your son cannot make you mad. Is that correct?"

"Correct."

"Mrs. Wagner, who actually says your words? Who creates the words that come out of your mouth?"

"I do."

"If that is the case, your husband cannot make you say one thing or the other. If you have chosen to say something, it has been your choice."

"That is true."

"Now, I am going to tell you why you are changed. You now know that you do your own thinking. You choose your own thoughts. You choose your own feelings and you say your own words. You now know that you own and control all the tools that are used to control your Subconscious that, in turn, controls your body. You are in 100% control, like it or not. So, what are you going to choose to think, feel, and say? Only good things, right?"

They both respond, "Right!"

"The next question that you may ask is when is all of this good stuff going to happen. The world misled you again, especially when it came to "time." They failed to explain the truth about time. I am going to tell you what real time is. First of all, let's draw an imaginary line on the ground. Let's say that one side of the line is the PAST and the other side of the line is the FUTURE. The line itself represents NOW. Mr. Wagner, based on the way that you were taught to think, does the PAST exist? Yes or no?"

"Yes."

"Incorrect. You say the PAST does exist. Go get me the tickets to last night's ball game. We already know the score. We will fly to Las Vegas and pawn everything that we own and place our bets on the winner. Then we will come back, watch the game and then go collect our money. We will do this with every good game in the past. Now, tell me, Mr. Wagner, does the PAST really exist? Yes or no?"

"No, but what about in my mind?"

"Those are only memories of the PAST, not the PAST itself."

"I cannot forget about the PAST, and that is what is bothering me most of all."

"That is a true statement. You cannot forget any information recorded in the Memory Bank, but you can choose simply not to recall. If you make the information unimportant to you, you will simply not recall the information, until you purposely call for it. The purpose is to only recall the good things for the "feel-good." It would be foolish to recall the bad things for the "feel-bad."

The only way to classify the bad information that is stored in the Memory Bank is to classify it as information for your protection, and not as bad information. If you classify it as bad, when you do think of it, you will get a "feel-bad." If you classify it as just information for your protection, there will be no "feel-bad" attached. Mrs. Wagner, does the FUTURE exist? Yes or no?"

"Yes, I hope so."

"Wrong again. If the FUTURE does exist, go get me the tickets and score of tonight's playoff game. You say the FUTURE does exist. That means that the score of that game does exist. Go get the score and the tickets and we will be off to Las Vegas to place our bets. You and I are going to run the world, because we will have all the money. You say the FUTURE does exist. Where is it?"

"People, the only time that does exist is a time frame called NOW. Every second of your life, you will spend in the time called NOW. The PAST does not exist and the FUTURE for us may exist when it gets here, but it does not exist NOW. I could call you on the phone in ten years and ask you what time it is, and you could respond that it is NOW, and you would be correct. You are always in a time frame called NOW. If you worry about the FUTURE or the PAST, that means you are worrying about something that does not exist. It is smart to plan for the FUTURE, so when it gets here, you will be prepared, but it is stupid to worry about something that does not exist. Tomorrow does not exist. When it gets here, it will be a NOW. The key is to command the Subconscious in NOW terms, such as: *I am*, or *I am not*, instead of *I want to be* or *I wish I had*.

"So, what are the good commands to your Subconscious? Let me say the commands for you and then you repeat them to yourself. Remember, this procedure doesn't require your belief or your acceptance. The Subconscious requires the proper word pattern or thought pattern. This is purely a word game between two different levels of the mind. If you do not command the Subconscious, it will command you, and it will use old, out of date and possibly untrue information.

Here are the commands." (You there, yes, you, the one who is reading this book. The one that has been listening in on our conversation. You, also, repeat the commands in your mind.)

"I am calm.
I am relaxed.
Nothing bothers me." *(That is a statement of fact, because nothing can bother you. You choose your own feelings.)*
"I am healthy.

I am happy.
I am attractive." *(Everybody is different, so you might as well call yourself good-looking.)*
"I am a genius." *(Every human mind works the same way. It records and gives back information. The only difference between you and Einstein is the different type of information and the way that information is given back. If you call yourself a genius, you will get better results than if you call yourself a dummy.)*
"I like myself first." *(You were told that you could not do that. You were told that was being egotistical and it was sinful. I do not think Jesus ever told a person not to think highly of himself. You must put yourself first. That way you get the "feel-goods" and you can stay healthy and help those you love. If you put yourself last, you are going to have the "feel-bads." You may wind up sick in the hospital and no good to anyone. If you put yourself first with you, that means you can take the end of the line and still feel good. I do not say I put my God first. But, my God lives within me; therefore, when I put myself first, I automatically put my God first. Do not write me and talk about religion, because I will simply throw your letters in the trash. Write me about the good changes in your life. Got it?)*

"Mr. and Mrs. Wagner, I ask you now: 'Are you changed?' You must say yes. If you say yes, you open the door for change. The command must be made before you can expect to get a response. Are you changed? Yes or no?"

"YES"

"YES"

"See there, you feel better already. You have been sitting there, analyzing me because you were trained to do so. You have been wondering, figuring, doubting, and sometimes arguing with me in your mind. Tomorrow I am going to put you on the couch and give you some good commands, but when you are not in my office, who is responsible for giving you the good commands? You are. Right?"

"Right," they both answered.

"And, if someone walks up to you and accidentally or intentionally puts the bad word on you, all you have to do is say, "NO" in your mind. They will never know the difference.

Mr. and Mrs. Wagner, now as you leave my office from this first visit, if one of you hears the other make a negative command, do not say, 'You are being negative,' or 'You said something wrong.' Whenever you say, 'You are being negative,' this is nothing more than a command to continue being negative. So, when you hear the accidental negative command, keep your mouth shut, as though you never heard it. That goes for both of you. I am being strong with you, because that is the only way to do this and get favorable results."

As the Wagners leave the office, I know that they will be like innumerable others that have come into my office. They changed, here in my office, and the changes are being put into effect, right now!

Tomorrow, when they come back, I will talk with them individually. I will take them back through their lives and explain to them why they had their "feel-bads" in each and every case. You can do this for yourself by taking every negative event and giving your Subconscious some sort of a reason for the happening. One of the best reasons that can be applied is: people were born knowing nothing. The things they did were because they thought they were right. They were not trained to think; they were taught to react.

So, you might as well choose not to recall the unpleasant things and choose to think about the fun things. Also, when thinking about the future, plan only good things. Planning is smart and worrying is stupid. Remember, you are a genius. All human beings are. Geniuses plan. They simply do not worry.

A young lady came in my office one day and she said that she needed to get her worrying organized! Now you know why there are so many hospitals and pharmacies!

The first chapter is a recap of what I have asked the Wagners to read overnight. It is simply a brief of this chapter. You must read it until this information becomes second nature to you. (Second nature means an automatic response by the Subconscious.)

Other chapters in this book talk about how to deal with specific situations. There are chapters about actual people and their situations. Read on. It gets even more interesting.

In the back of this book, you will find an Order Blank, in case you would like to hear some of my great advice on audiocassette.

A friend told me, before I got into this business, that my voice was not right for this type of work. Look at me now! I am the world's greatest hypnotist! And guess what? Hypnosis, as you understood it, does not exist, but perfect concentration does!

NOTES

CHAPTER 4

STRESS IS A FEELING AND FEELINGS ARE A CHOICE

I am sure you have heard it said many times that a person's health is the result of his state of mind. It is a fact that the Subconscious Mind controls the body functions and, in the process, produces certain feelings based on the thoughts of the individual. Again, if the person thinks or talks constantly about uncomfortable situations and uncomfortable conditions, he will soon develop uncomfortable feelings. These uncomfortable feelings will show up in the form of various symptoms: stomach ache, pain, cancer, diseases of all kinds, nail biting, over-eating or smoking, to mention a few. On the other hand, if a person eliminates uncomfortable thoughts, worry and stress from his mind, then his body is given permission to be 100% healthy.

There is absolutely no such thing as stress on your body, unless you create it. One man does a job and indicates he feels stress, as a result of his job. Another man can do the same job and find it to be a pleasure. Along the same line, it would be unwise to worry. The smart person plans. And he plans only good things. It would be foolish to plan disaster. Some people merely think too much about things they cannot control, and then they call it "worry." The Subconscious Mind accepts the words literally. Therefore, when someone says, "I work in a stressful setting," or "I worry about my job and my family," the words and thoughts will do him harm. That person should be saying, "There are many things happening at the office," or "I care about my family, but I am 100% relaxed. I am 100% healthy, and I am

Number One. I can handle any situation."

Sickness is not necessary. It is a fact that sickness is usually brought on by the way we think, with the possible exception of certain situations, such as staph infections, cross-infections, etc. One of these days, I will do a research paper on the ability of the human body and mind to overcome cross-infections, by using the Subconscious to control the body functions. If the body is controlled by the Subconscious, and the Subconscious is controlled by the Conscious, there is absolutely no need to be sick!

You were taught all the wrong things to say. You were taught all the wrong things to do. You were taught that stress does exist, even though the rack (the ultimate in stress!) was done away with in the early 13th century. The thumbscrew has been outlawed. There is no such thing as "pressure," unless you create it yourself. If the Subconscious Mind accepts words literally, you must be very, very careful how you think and what you say.

You were literally trained in a negative world. This training was not intentionally negative; people just did not know the difference. Now that you understand that the Subconscious Mind controls the body functions and that you can consciously control the Subconscious Mind, you can be 100% healthy. If you are in a situation or relationship with another person, the way you think, the way you talk and the way you act, generally determine the outcome of the relationship. A person might say, "My wife just drives me crazy. My mother-in-law is a pain in the neck. My children are killing me." Even though these statements may be said in jest, remember, the Subconscious Mind accepts the words literally, and sure enough, the person is going crazy; he has a pain in his neck; and he is dying; all as a result of the way he thinks and speaks.

If the Subconscious Mind controls the body and you choose your own feelings, as a result of the way you think, then absolutely nothing can bother you; absolutely nothing can upset you; and nothing can make you mad. If the Subconscious Mind understands the words literally, maybe you should look at the meaning of the words you use. "Mad" comes from "mad dog; sick; foaming at the mouth; dying." Where do we get the word, " upset"? From "upside down; not right side up." Where do we get the word, "problem"? From "math class; school."

It is o.k. to like a situation, or it is o.k. not to like a situation. But why is it necessary to become "upset; to get mad; to become violent, tense, under pressure," or to have "problems"? The Subconscious Mind will take all these negative thoughts and produce uncomfortable feelings. Often times, you can go to the doctor, and the doctor will identify the problem by saying, "Your kidneys don't work," for example, instead of identifying the actual problem. In reality, he has only recognized the symptoms. The problem is the information received by the body from the Subconscious Mind.

If the body will, in fact, respond to Subconscious commands as a result of Conscious logic, then it is possible that the kidneys can return to normal, or any other body function can be re-instated. (I will discuss a kidney disease case in a later chapter.) When the Subconscious Mind has been told that the body is healthy, the body repairs itself. When you get a cut on the hand, you don't repair it with staples, glue, or cellophane tape. The body repairs itself. So, by commanding the body, we become 100% healthy.

The way we have been taught to think has produced

an unhealthy society. Everywhere you look, you will see new hospitals being built. That ought to tell you something. This negative teaching was not done intentionally, as I said before. People taught the best they knew. In fact, as far back as 2000 years ago, one man said, "The way you think in your heart, you will become." And it appears as though the man knew what he was talking about. The only problem was that 12 men walked away with 12 different opinions, and then there were 144 different opinions, and now there are thousands of different churches, all trying to do the same thing.

The body produces certain feelings, as a result of certain information that has gone into the Subconscious Mind. That, we have already determined. The Subconscious Mind and/or our Memory Bank was designed to help us, not to hurt us. The Subconscious Mind remembers that fire is hot. It tells us to keep our distance, so that we don't get burned. It also tells us that fire is hot, so that we can get warm if we don't like the cold. The Subconscious Mind and the Memory Bank are designed to protect us.

For instance, whenever we receive a message from the Subconscious Mind that comes in the form of nervousness, or an uncomfortable feeling, it is an indication that there may be something in our environment that the Subconscious thinks is no good. If information were not recorded in our Memory Banks about poisonous snakes, we might try to handle the wrong kind of snake and possibly get bitten. So, the Subconscious works to protect us.

A simple example would be this situation. An individual takes his lunch break under a shade tree, and after his lunch, he decides to take a nap. While taking his nap, a brick falls out of the tree and hits him on the head. The man

Stress Is A Feeling and Feelings Are A Choice

jumps up. He is mad and he is hurt. He looks up in the tree and sees nothing that caused the brick to fall out of the tree, and there is no one around for miles. The Subconscious has experienced a situation it does not understand. The next day, he is on a new job site. He sees a tree. He decides to sit down and have lunch, but he checks the tree first. A little uneasy, he goes ahead and sits down and has his lunch. Having inspected the tree, he feels secure and decides to take a nap. Another brick falls out of the tree and hits him on the head. He jumps up, confused, and very hurt, because the brick hit him in the same spot and it was sore from the day before. By now, he is really confused.

The third day, there is a tree, a different job site, and again, no one within miles. It is 110 degrees out in the sun and he would like to sit underneath the shade tree and have his lunch, but he is not going to sit under that tree, because he knows he will be hit in the head with another brick. So he avoids sitting under trees altogether. A few moments later, some friends come by and say, "Let's have lunch under that tree, and after lunch, let's take a nap." The man says, "No! I've been hurt before. I do not want to be hurt again." His friends are determined and answer, "We are going to take you over and put you under the tree. We want you out of the sun. We are trying to help you." The man fights his friends off with everything he has, but they overpower him and take him to the tree. Then, the Subconscious Mind begins to produce nervousness, fear, uncomfortable feelings, and all-around hysterical feelings, because the Subconscious Mind thinks he is going to get hit in the head with another brick.

Now, when dealing with uncomfortable feelings in a particular situation, the Conscious Mind can override the Subconscious Mind by saying, "I am in control; I choose my own feelings. If a brick starts to fall out of the tree, I will just step aside. This very moment, absolutely nothing bothers me. I control my life; I do my own thinking." As a result, he is back in control of his feelings. When he realizes that the two bricks were only from those first two trees, he can simply protect himself when being around those two particular trees. There is no need for "feel-bads."

Man's health is determined by how and what he thinks. How and what are you going to think? Only good things! Right!

COMMENTS FROM CLIENTS

Recently, I was a client of yours at your office and here are a few comments I would like to share with you. An ad that appeared in the paper triggered this chain of actions:
1. Call for an appointment
2. Private consultation and discussions regarding the "whys" we are overweight
3. A more workable knowledge of the power of the mind and the need for self-control in our present society, and a more workable, optimistic "attitude" on my present way of life.

So very impressed was I that I returned to your office with my husband, Charles, for the very same reasons. After Charles returned home from his very first session with you, there was a very noticeable change in his attitude and character. You see, the Charles who came with me on his first session, was a very crude, hostile, selfish, insensitive and uncaring husband and father, who had absolutely no self-confidence, even though he was a medical doctor. I literally watched him become a very pleasant, protective, and even friendly person overnight. Within two weeks, he began doing things for me and the children, I had never dreamed possible. He became aware and attentive of me as a wife. Took the children out to movies and dinner. Bought our daughter her graduation ring half a year early. He began to do household duties and what is considered wifely chores, and he even bought me a car in my name, so that I would have a family back-up car during his absence away from home.

Actually what I am trying to say, Tom, is that you're the best alchemist in Texas. I know I brought to your office, a "Frog," but the man I now know has become a living, expressing "Prince."

As for me, when I first came to see you, I was not at the center of my being, as I had known myself to be. I could no longer command the 4 "W's" in all of life's expression. And, while I could write a page of each of the "W's,"* simplified and instantly, now I have the knowledge of them at my command for use of them in all of my daily activities, which keeps me aware and relaxed in any and every situation. You see, simplified, I now know who am I, what am I, where am I, why am I.

    I am to create.
    I am to assist.
    I am to love and be loved.
    I am to give and receive.
    I am to understand.
    I am to befriend.
    I am to express.

And, etc., etc., etc., as this list is infinite, and all this came through intuitively after our second session. Simply talking "with" you expanded my consciousness to be applied in all creations. Both action and reaction, where applicable.

Now, here comes the really good stuff and this is true. You are a beautiful person, loaded with charisma. Surely Heaven blesses your mission.

I don't recall this lady discussing the 4 W's, whatever they are or whatever they mean. She must have gotten them from some other program. If it works for her, I'm all for it. I think this lady was very nice, but a little overly reactive about my participation in her and her husband's change of attitudes and lifestyle. All I did was give her information, nothing more, nothing less. I was just the messenger. She used the information and got good results. Now, it's your turn. *Either use the information or continue to be as you are. (Keep on reading!)*

* * *

Before I came to you and underwent hypnosis,* I was a very unhappy person. I was unhappy with myself, mainly. Because I was overweight and my face was all broken out, I had a very low self-esteem. I had been to a dermatologist for my face before and it didn't seem to help any. In only one week's time, after being hypnotized, my face looks clearer than it has in months. I was letting things bother me for no reason and keeping it all inside and it was trying to come out through my face. I now see myself in a better light and also look at other things around me differently. I am now content with the way I am and the way I will be when I reach my goal.

I no longer let the actions or words of others hinder me. I care about myself first and, therefore, I can be able to care for someone else. And, it was all right there, in my subconscious all the time. I wish someone had shown me how to use the positive attitudes about everything before now.

*The person was never hypnotized. She was in a state of perfect relaxation and perfect concentration. I gave her positive suggestions; that's all.

* * *

I feel this is the beginning of becoming relaxed, for the first time in twenty-five years.

* * *

Your method has helped me with a physical problem. My previous orientation had been in passive relaxation and meditation, which helped to some degree, but had no "carry-over" effect in my everyday life. At first, your active relaxation seemed rather authoritarian, but it works. You said, "You will do as I say. You are healthy, etc." You allow no room for negative thoughts. You have taught me to control my body and my life. The method is not a blind denial of negatives, but rather, learning that you need not choose them for yourself.

My main message to those who might read this is that this method works quickly and does carry over into every aspect of my life.*
**Cha-ching! A new convert!*

* * *

My daughter had a personal situation before coming to you. She was down on herself. That is, she didn't think very highly of herself or others around her. She didn't try in schoolwork. Now, after seeing you, she thinks more positive. She likes herself and is more concerned about others. She works harder in school and is getting more involved in sports. You have helped her, tremendously.

My other daughter had a health situation. She was always worried about things that happened in the past and things that might happen. Now, she seems more relaxed and thinks better of herself. And, thinks positive. Speaks up in group sessions. Getting more involved. Doesn't seem to worry about her past history. She seems to have put that situation behind her. I think she'll be a much better school teacher and person now, having had these sessions with you.

These sessions have helped me as well, as a mother and person. I now realize some of the things I was doing and saying (I thought I was right) were wrong and situations were passed on to them. I am thinking more positive, now. I think we all three are in complete control now.

* * *

Since I was at your office, the world has not changed one bit, but I have. Using what you taught me, I can be calm in an instant, when I never was able to, before.

Using what you taught me, I have been able to apply my science of chiropractic much more efficiently, because of better concentration and bringing myself to the present.

* * *

I have learned a great deal about myself and the causes for a lot of my behavior. I have learned that I, and I alone, am responsible and in total control of my behavior. I feel that all this will lead to my making myself a happier and more fulfilled person.

* * *

NOTES

CHAPTER 5

PUT THE UNCOMFORTABLE PAST AWAY FOREVER

I do not classify my clients according to their ability to be hypnotized. In this chapter, I am going to turn around all theories on a person's ability to be hypnotized. The way I teach hypnosis is that each and every subject is a good subject, because I am the world's best hypnotist. It is unimportant that you know this fact, but it is important to me, because when I tell my Subconscious Mind that I am the best hypnotist, I always produce desirable results. I remember everything I read regarding hypnosis. I am the best hypnotic technician in the world today, only because I have conditioned myself to think that way.

The Subconscious Mind will be affected by the things that are said, the environment, and the general nature of things, no matter what age you are, unless you are in control of your Subconscious, as you should be. An example is a case of a 60-year old man who came to me. He explained that things just had not been right throughout his life. He had searched high and low for the answers to his uncomfortable feelings. He seemed to be a very knowledgeable person. He had graduated from a mid-western university and had been successful all of his life. But he still carried a feeling that he had some sort of mental block about being truly happy.

This man, like other clients, accepted suggestion very well. After visiting with this man, it was determined that when he was the age of 6 or 7, he had become ill, was taken to the hospital, and almost died. At the age of 21 or 22, he flunked out his senior year in college, as had his mother at that age. He eventually went back to school and received his degree. But, throughout his life, he recounted uncomfortable feelings that he could not explain.

In the age-regression process, the subject is taken back through time to the first day of his life. What basically happens here, is that the subject has the ability to remember easier when he is in that super-relaxed state. The information from Day One is recorded in your Subconscious Mind, much like a giant tape recorder. Every experience, every thought, every sensation is recorded, so it is very easy in this so-called hypnotic state to pull this information from the Subconscious Mind. And, in a later chapter, I will teach you to do that for yourself.

I took this man back to the age of two and he recounted an experience with his father. When the child was two years old, his father learned that his wife had developed an ovarian cyst that was possibly cancerous. Sixty years ago, cancer was even a more dreaded disease than it is today. Today it can be eliminated! The father saw a picture of instant death; losing his wife; and being left alone to raise a small child. The man was extremely distraught. He turned to the child and, without thinking, said to the two-year old, "You have caused your mother to be sick and she may die. If you had not been born, your mother would be well today. You are killing your mother."

Even though the child, at age two, did not understand the words, this information was recorded on the Subconscious tape recorder. As the child grew older, the words developed meaning. I feel this was the time that the Subconscious took a kick in the face. The Subconscious realized: "I'm killing my mother. I'm causing my mother to die. Had it not been for me, my mother would be well." Even though, consciously, the child knew his mother was o.k., subconsciously, he had the message that he was killing his mother. So, each and every time his mother coughed, felt bad, or felt uncomfortable, the child took a mental beating. Can you imagine the psychological impact on a person with this message recorded in the Memory Bank? What happened? Simply this. The Subconscious recorded information that it could not rationalize; therefore, creating uncomfortable feelings. This information needed to be turned around, or rationalized, so that the child could be free from those uncomfortable feelings.

I asked his Subconscious Mind, while in the super-relaxed state, "Was your father a doctor?" His Subconscious said, "No." I said, "Well then, forget it. The statement your father made was medically incorrect." I asked his Subconscious Mind, "How can a two year old child affect the health of another person?" His Subconscious responded, "Absolutely no way!" At that point, I said, "Forget it. The information meant nothing." In theory, what happened at this point is, his Subconscious said, "Thank God! I can put those thoughts away forever." This relieved his Subconscious of the need for an answer.

It makes no difference how you rationalize the comments you hear. You must rationalize them in order that the Subconscious does not take a mental beating. That is why it is so important to choose not to be bothered by anything, anybody, anywhere; or to choose not to be affected in any adverse way. The Subconscious responded when the above-mentioned mother just coughed or got sick, even though she did not die from that cancerous cyst. The Subconscious merely responded in an effort to warn the child that he was killing his mother. It responded with a symptom; a feeling; an uncomfortable sensation. That uncomfortable feeling was a sign that there was bad information in the Subconscious Mind. That is why it is so important to control your Subconscious, rather than to allow yourself to become negatively conditioned by your environment. You should determine your own conditioning, within the guidelines of our organized society.

At this point, it is very important to explain to you how to turn around the bad information in the Subconscious, so that you have only good information stored there. This information is so very, very important. You must listen and understand what I have to say. It makes no difference who you are or where you come from or what your physical status is. You must go to your Subconscious and put the uncomfortable past away forever. You cannot change the past. The past is like a broken egg, so you will put the uncomfortable past away forever and remember only the good times. If you could change the past, you would be a rich person. If you could predict the future, you would be in great demand. So, live for today. Make yourself happy today. Don't waste your time thinking of the uncomfortable past or worrying about the future. It is wise to plan for the future, because the Subconscious Mind understands planning to be a positive approach, but as you can see, it would be foolish to worry about the future. You are a human being and all human beings have the ability to think. A smart person like you, plans and does not worry. A smart person like you, remembers the good times of the past and does not waste his time thinking of the uncomfortable times.

You now understand that the Subconscious can only handle *yes* or *no*. It cannot handle *try*. Take notice of this following statement. If you try to make your Subconscious deal with the past, you will get a "feel-bad." It is o.k. to plan

Put the Uncomfortable Past Away For Ever

in the NOW for the future, so that you are prepared when it arrives and becomes a NOW. When the NOW becomes a PAST, it is no longer important.

Use these commands for eliminating the PAST: "I remember only the good times from the past. Anything that happened in the past that was a negative that I don't understand is of no value to me. It is totally unimportant. I am happy and healthy. I plan only beautiful, happy things for the future. Nothing bothers me. If I make concessions, I have freedom of thought and mind. I think only happy, healthy thoughts."

We have become conditioned by our environment. So, I now say to you to stop that conditioning and be in control of your own life. That is the way it was meant to be. Your creator designed you to be perfect. Think of yourself that way. And your Subconscious will make you that way!

COMMENTS FROM A CLIENT

I have really enjoyed your program because of the idea of being able to control your feelings and attitudes. It is great to know that you are responsible for your feelings and can make them what you want. Knowing this has helped me see that I am more independent of others and of circumstances, in that I can respond to them in the way I really want. I can be the person I want to be, regardless of the situations around me. It is also a relief to be able to let go of the unpleasant things in the past and forget them, so that they have no influence on me, now. I like knowing that it is best to live the present and let the future fall into place, as it comes, without worrying about it.

* * *

CHAPTER 6

A LOOK AT DEPRESSION

Depression is simply a feeling, and feelings are a simple choice. I'm sure that you're sitting there thinking that YOU never chose to be depressed, or pressured, or to feel stress. I am here to tell you that the only way you could have experienced depression was to have created it yourself. As I told you in previous chapters, you were not taught to think. You were taught purely to react. They may have told you that if certain things happened, it would be depressing. I am telling you that if certain things happen, they just happen. These actions have nothing to do with your psychological state. Even if you were to say that losing a leg would be depressing, I disagree. If the leg is gone, the rest of the body is still the same. The time is NOW. The leg is not there NOW. How can you go on about your life, if you are depressed about something that does not exist? The leg does not exist. It would be foolish also, to be depressed about the fact that you are missing one leg. There is nothing you can do about the missing leg, so why be depressed about something that you can do nothing about.

There was a young man in my office just yesterday, and he said that he was depressed and he did not know why. He came into the office and sat down and started to command his Subconscious. Let us take a look at the man's exact words, "I am not happy with myself." Remember, the command is made when *I, me, my, myself, we, us, our,* is used with a definite *yes* or *no*. The Subconscious is also defined as *self* and the man has just commanded his Subconscious to not like itself. The Subconscious simply does as it is commanded and sends the appropriate feeling. In this case, if you don't like *self*, then *self* will send you a "feel-bad." It is foolish not to like *self*. Oh, remember they told you that liking *self* was a sin. I do not think Jesus ever said not to like yourself. I think, if you look in your Bible, Jesus said that if you did something that wasn't good, to just not do it again and to forget it.

My client said, "I have no desire to work." The Subconscious has been told not to take him to work. If he goes to work, he puts himself in a *yes* and *no* situation, and the Subconscious cannot handle *yes* and *no* at the same time. How many people do you know go to work every day and complain about their jobs? That doesn't sound too logical to me. If you go to work, love it. If you stay home, love that. But, simply do not go to work and complain about having to go. By the way, if you do not go to work, you may not make any money and you may starve to death. That is your choice. If you choose to starve to death, that leaves more room for those that enjoy living.

"My stomach stays in a bundle of nerves." Whenever you feel that uncomfortable feeling in your stomach that has been sent to you by your preconditioned Subconscious, you must say in your mind: "Relax, relax, relax. I am always relaxed." Then. the body will approach a relaxed state. After a while, the Subconscious will become reconditioned to relaxation, under those circumstances.

"I have lost my effectiveness," he said. That is a lie. You cannot lose your effectiveness. You have just stopped using it. It is still there. Remember, everything that you have ever experienced is still there.

"I have no outside interests." The Subconscious says, "Let's do nothing."

"By Tuesday, I am a nervous wreck." The Subconscious knows when Tuesday is. So, on Tuesday, the Subconscious is going to send him an even worse feeling.

"I stay nervous." The Subconscious says, "Let's stay nervous."

Folks, do you get the point? You had better watch your mouth and your thoughts when you are thinking or talking about *I, me, my, myself*.

A lady who claimed she had been depressed for about 17 years, came to my office. She said she had been seeing her shrink once a week for 17 years. Each week after her visit, the doctor would tell her that she was still depressed, and she did not say "NO."

Whenever you hear a command that you do not like, you must say or think "NO" or it becomes an automatic command to be carried out at a later date. When you say "NO," you must give the reverse command, such as the following, "I am happy and nothing is going to change that. I am healthy and I am going to stay that way, etc." Your Subconscious will pick up on the new command and it will start sending you happy and healthy feelings. When your Subconscious tries to send you a lousy feeling, you must be aware of it and immediately eliminate it with a favorable command.

You don't need depression. Eliminate it!

COMMENTS FROM CLIENTS

I sleep better since learning to use my subconscious. I am more relaxed, calmer in nature. By that, I mean my reasoning is faster and I am able to make and think about my decisions on matters of family interest or personal interest with more determination. I have not had a depressed day since I began your program. I go to sleep at night with the Relaxation tape on my pillow and fall fast asleep much more quickly. I enjoyed reading Dr. Atkins' Diet Book that you recommended and find that it is a diet* that will work for me.

I take things as they come along and what I cannot change, I learn to live with. I am grateful for your help.

I don't think anybody should be on a diet. Today, the word, "diet," has progressed to mean "something troublesome to do; a difficult thing; a negative association." Why not think or say, "I have simply changed the way I think and eat"? By the way, you do need to know the chemistry of foods and how they affect the body.

* * *

I had excellent results. You did more for me in 2 hours than I had been able to do for myself in months. The hypnosis made it possible for me to put my life in perspective and gain control of my emotions.

* * *

It was very difficult for me to make an appointment with you. When I called and explained my problem, I felt "cheap." But I was desperate. I had contemplated leaving town or simply "running away." I felt alone, insecure, and very depressed.

After my first visit, I could not believe the change. I was extremely happy. So happy that I started singing. I felt alive again. After the second visit, I began to feel less excited, but realistically content. I felt and do feel like a real person. A strong, confident real person. I know now that I am in control of my life. I "slipped" once. But, when I regained my composure, I felt stronger than ever before. I still feel lonely sometimes, but I know that I can do something to change that feeling--if I CHOOSE TO!

* * *

Life is great these days, thanks to you. One year ago, I came to your office for a visit. Since then, I have lost 40 pounds, by myself, without medication or repeated visits. You're better than a doctor and less expensive. Also, I had psoriasis of the scalp and face, which has been a nuisance for the past twenty years. It was difficult to wear makeup. What an improvement, almost immediately. It's terrific what hypnosis can do.

Before visiting your office, I was depressed, I'd say 50% of the time and wanted to run away from my problems. In the last year, I've never thought of running away from situations. I've added new words to my vocabulary that will help me solve the situations. Life is great with me, Tom. Now, it's worth living.

* * *

Since I have seen you, I feel that I understand myself, as well as others, better. I feel better about myself and feel I can handle situations a lot better than before I saw you. I enjoy life more now and feel more relaxed. I have seen a change within myself and feel it's all for the good of myself. I am pleased with my sessions and am glad that I did see you. I'm also happy that there is someone who can show people that they can handle situations, if they really want to. Thanks, again.

* * *

Before my sessions with you, I allowed myself to be dictated to; had doubts about myself; at times, no self-confidence; depressions; self-pity; gained weight; and was tremendously displeased with myself.
This is only my third session and already, I like myself. I am speaking out, and taking action on my part, when needed. I have more confidence and my whole attitude towards people, things in general, and my life, is changing. I am much happier. My weight is going down, but that seems only a small goal, compared to the other accomplishments.

* * *

I just do not know how to express my gratitude for the transformation that you made out of me. I am a different person since I saw you. Now, I am the best. I am Number One.
I am very sorry that I did not know about you before I went to see several psychiatrists out of the state of Texas

and in the state of Texas. The first psychiatrist that I saw was not concerned about my feelings, but only about the level of Aventil in my blood. I spent between hospital fees and doctors' fees (psychiatrists and psychologists) no less than three thousand dollars. I could not do my work because my hands used to shake to the point that I was embarrassed to do anything in front of another person. I saw the first psychiatrist daily for three weeks, and at the end of the three weeks, I felt worse than when I first saw him. Then, I saw two other psychiatrists. I improved considerably with the last one, but the complete transformation came after I saw you.

* * *

It is a wonderful feeling to be healthy after feeling so bad for so long.

* * *

NOTES

CHAPTER 7

SMOKING CAN'T KILL YOU, BUT NOT THINKING AND THE LACK OF OXYGEN CAN

Smoking is very much like putting charcoal briquettes in a paper sack. The smoke is like a piece of carbon. If you put enough briquettes in a small sack, there is no room for air. Once the carbon gets in the lungs, the body secretes a fluid to protect itself from the carbon particles. That's what you cough up when you smoke. After a while, there is simply no room for the air or oxygen. After you stop smoking, the lungs start to clear, but it takes quite some time. Also, without adequate oxygen, the body cannot overcome the toxins and poisons in the tobacco. The body cells break down, then lung cancer and heart disease appear. Quitting smoking will allow the body a chance to repair itself.

Would you like to quit smoking? Giving up smoking is one of the easiest things in the world to do. But the world has conditioned you into thinking that quitting smoking is a most difficult, if not impossible, procedure.

About one-tenth of my business comes from people who want to quit smoking. I think that it would be safe to say that 100% of those people come into my office thinking that their problem is their inability to give up the weed, but when they lay their cards on the table, the real problem has to do with something totally different.

The problem generally has to do with the person's inability to deal with a situation; either at work, at home, or in some other close relationship. When the person sees, in his mind, the negative side of the situation, the Subconscious records the negative and then produces an uncomfortable feeling. As I have said earlier, the Subconscious is designed to take care of you. When the "feel-bad" is experienced, as a result of the negative thought, the Subconscious simply attempts to take the person to something that it thinks will cause a "feel-good." You have heard many times, "Have a cigarette and relax." Billboards show the following: a sensuous-looking lady, lounging around in her whatevers, smoking a cigarette; or a strong, handsome man on the back of a beautiful horse, overlooking some of the most breathtaking country in the world, smoking his favorite brand of cigarettes. And the list goes on. The advertising agency people know that you were not trained to think. They know that you were trained to react, like an animal; so they've got you. Well, they had you until the time you bought this book. Now you know how to think, and you no longer react like an animal. You think like an intelligent, rational, logical human being. You are no longer subject to other peoples' suggestions. You hear what they have to say, but you make up your own mind.

At this point and time, if you are smoking, or if you are a smoker and you want to quit, you are to simply say to yourself, in your mind, "I have stopped smoking." If you have a cigarette in your hand, PUT IT OUT NOW! If you have cigarettes in your pocket or purse, GO THROW THEM AWAY!

In fact, PUT THIS BOOK DOWN and go through everything that you own! Take all of the cigarettes you have in your possession; put them in a brown paper bag, and tie or tape it closed. When you have done this, return to reading this chapter. DO EXACTLY AS I SAY! DO IT RIGHT NOW! You have stopped smoking, as of RIGHT NOW! DO IT! GET UP AND DO IT!

Do not continue to read the remaining part of this chapter until you have done as I have asked you to do.

I want you to repeat the following to yourself: "I have done it. I have stopped smoking. I have finally made up my mind. I no longer smoke. I am very relaxed not smoking. Now, I am always relaxed."

Now turn back to Chapter 2 and repeat the positive commands that I have outlined for you at the end of the chapter. Then, repeat the above command several more times. After you have done this, continue to read this chapter.

Let me tell you how your government and the news media have been giving you the "Tennessee Shuffle." The Surgeon General has determined that cigarettes are even more dangerous than was previously thought. Then, he gives you the command that no one has found an easy way for people to stop smoking. So, what does the public continue to do? SMOKE, SMOKE, SMOKE!

If the Surgeon General would just say, "Cigarettes are even more dangerous than we previously thought, and we have found a sure-fire, easy way to give up cigarettes. You can do it by simply putting down your cigarettes and repeating to yourself that you no longer smoke and that you are totally relaxed not smoking." Most people would then do so. This, of course, would cripple the tobacco industry and the government is not going to do that. So WHO has been manipulating whom? NOT ANY MORE! You have simply stopped smoking and it is very easy not to smoke.

Later, your Subconscious might try to get you to have a cigarette, if you accidentally think negatively. So, if this happens, simply over-rule your Subconscious and repeat the following, "No, thank you. I do not smoke. I am relaxed and happy not smoking." You MUST do this because now YOU control your Subconscious. It does not control you.

If you are smoking, it is obvious that you are not thinking. Simply do not smoke or drink, and use your head to become relaxed. How do you feel now that you no longer smoke? You must respond to your Subconscious: "It is fantastic! I feel great! I feel wonderful!" Remember, you choose your own feelings, so choose only good feelings.

The way you give up smoking is to simply put down your cigarettes and not smoke. I must have had 500 people tell me that they cannot do that. They cannot just put down their cigarettes. Many have said that they are slaves to cigarettes and that smoking is the only way they know how to relax. They tell me that they have to smoke a cigarette with their coffee. They have to smoke a cigarette after a meal, and so on. Now, review the commands that they have given their Subconscious Minds. They have told their Subconscious Minds to continue smoking, and that is exactly what is going to happen.

If you put down your cigarettes and say, "I am not going to smoke a cigarette, but I sure would like to have one," the Subconscious Mind is going to pay off like a slot machine! With these thoughts, you are sure to return to smoking. Again, you are saying, "I want the cigarette. It is tough to give up smoking and I am trying to quit." Your Subconscious, in turn, says, "You are right. It is tough. You are only *trying* and *trying* doesn't get it."

Remember, the Subconscious only understands *yes* or *no*. Either you smoke or you do not smoke. You must give to yourself and think to yourself, the following commands: "I do not smoke and I will not take another cigarette. I feel good not smoking. It is very easy now that I no longer smoke. I am relaxed not smoking and when I am with my friends, I have more fun not smoking. I do my own thinking. I am happy as a non-smoker. When someone offers me a cigarette, I simply say, 'No, thank you. I do not smoke.' If I am in a room full of people and they are smoking, their smoke will not bother me in any way. I simply do not smoke."

If you say, "I cannot say these words," you and I both know you are lying. What you must do first, is to say the words. So, say the words. Then, put yourself in that super-relaxed state and say the words again. Now, if at anytime, you say to yourself, "The words are not true," the Subconscious Mind will say, "You are correct. They are not true." Remember that what you put into the Subconscious, you will get out in the form of an action or a feeling. So, you will say, in your mind, "The words are true."

Let us assume that you and I are going camping and you asked me to stop by the store to purchase a carton of your favorite cigarettes. I do not smoke, so I decide to help you give up smoking. While I am in the store buying your carton of cigarettes, I take out all of the cigarettes and put a block of wood in the carton and seal it back up. When I return to the car where we have our camping gear packed, you are pleased to see that I have purchased a carton of your brand of cigarettes.

While we are on our camping trip, I have noticed that you have only 3 cigarettes left in your shirt pocket. But, you are happy, thinking that you have 3 cigarettes left, plus a new carton. We take off for the mountains. It is a beautiful day. You are happy. You have a cigarette. Now you have only 2 cigarettes left, because you have just finished one. But you are happy. You think that you have 2 cigarettes, plus a full carton.

We get halfway to the mountains. It is a beautiful day and we expect to be in the mountains for the long, three-day weekend. You have another cigarette. Now you have only 1 cigarette left. But you are happy. You think that you have 1 cigarette and a full carton. We get to the campsite. You have your last cigarette and we are eight hours away from the nearest store. You are not concerned, because you think that you still have a full carton of cigarettes.

After the evening meal, you decide to have another cigarette. You go to the car, take out the carton of cigarettes and open it. SURPRISE! SURPRISE! A block of wood! At this point in time, because of your negative way of thinking, you simply choose to blow your cool! Three days on vacation without your cigarettes! What are you going to do? Bear in mind, it wasn't the cigarettes that kept you happy, while driving to the mountains. It was the thought that you had a carton of cigarettes that kept you happy. Cigarettes do not have power. They do only one thing: prevent you from thinking straight. It was the thought that you had cigarettes that kept you happy, not the cigarettes themselves.

By changing the way you think and changing the way you reinforce your thinking about cigarettes, you simply do not smoke. If you say to yourself, "I cannot change the way I think," you do not fool me or anyone else. We both know that you and only you, do your thinking. If that is the case, you simply think as though you are a non-smoker. As you can see, it is very easy now that you have given up your cigarettes, because NOW you are a non-smoker.

If you say, "I am trying to quit smoking," the door is left open to have another cigarette. Either you have quit or you have not. Make up your mind. Again, the Subconscious only understands *yes* or *no*.

Now that you have quit smoking, you will reinforce to your Subconscious Mind that you are a completely relaxed, healthy, happy human being. And when you hear someone say, "I am trying to quit smoking and I am a nervous wreck," you can smile and say, "I do not smoke and I am relaxed, healthy, and happy." By actually saying the words first, you begin to think the words. You will say to yourself, "The words are true." Then you will begin to understand and know that what you are saying is fact.

Add the following statements to your commands to Self: "I do not even remember what it was like to smoke and I do not even think about cigarettes anymore." These commands to Self will keep you from thinking about cigarettes. If there is no thought, there will be no command. Remember, simple thoughts can be simple commands.

When someone asks you how you feel now that you have quit, you must respond with the answers that are going to get you the best feelings, such as, "I feel great now that I have quit. It was easy to give up the cigarettes." That person will probably think in his mind, "I wish I could be that strong and that in-control." You know it is all in the way you think and speak and command Self. Keep it simple, because it is.

Congratulations, Non-Smoker!

COMMENTS FROM CLIENTS

Just to let you know and to thank you for helping me celebrate one year of not needing a cigarette.

* * *

Since my first visit, I have been able to relax, and feel 100% better. I was able to stop smoking without any effort or discomfort at all. I'm very glad to have taken this course because I know the benefits derived are outstanding!

* * *

CHAPTER 8

THROW THE BEAR A COOKIE

Let's assume for a moment that you have a grizzly bear living in your backyard. If you go into the backyard, take a baseball bat and hit the bear in the head with it, you're going to have a fight on your hands. The bear will not stand for that type of treatment. Let's say that you went down to the local supermarket and purchased a package of bear cookies. You know, the great big ones next to the dog biscuits. Now that you have purchased the cookies, take the cookies and the baseball bat and go back into the yard where you keep your pet grizzly bear. The whole idea is to get the bear to do as he is told. First, pitch the bear a cookie. Wait until he picks up the cookie and starts to eat it. Then, hit him with the baseball bat. Before the bear can fight you, he will have to put down the cookie. If it is a good cookie, he will take the punch. If not, you lose!

I have done this to you many times during the writing of this book. I threw you the cookie and then threw you the punch. Example: "You are a wise and intelligent person. Simply do as I have advised in this book." A person will not turn on himself and admit that he is not wise and intelligent. Therefore, he accepts the entire statement. Because people were not trained to stop and think before they act and speak, the average person will accept the command, in order to keep the cookies. Example: My boys' pickup truck needed a new bearing on one of the rear axles. The process takes about thirty seconds, but a large press is required to press off the old bearing and press on the new. I bought a new bearing and took the bearing and axle into the machine shop to have it pressed. As I walked up to the counter, I could see that the machinist looked as though he had swallowed a handful of nails. He looked like the "Grinch that stole Christmas"!

As he came up to the counter, I said, "Say, they tell me next door at the parts house that you are the resident genius-in-charge. They say that you know more about this machine shop than anybody. Could you press this bearing on this axle for me while I wait?" He yanked that axle and bearing out of my hands, went over to the press, and in about 30 to 45 seconds, he had done the job. I paid him $5.00 and I was out the door.

I was on my lunch hour and had I rushed into the shop and said, "I am on my lunch hour and I am in a big hurry. Could you press this axle and bearing for me?" He could have said, "Say, it is lunch time. I had better go to lunch, too." By my using a small bit of information that may or may not have been true, I said something nice to the man and it probably made his day. Use this procedure on everybody. You will be surprised how people will react to something favorable that is said about them.

Now, you have been reading this book and this particular chapter. I know you are basically a good person and you are a person that has a fantastic mind. Do as I recommend in this book. See, I got you! You do not want to argue with my last statement. It works. So, use it!

Many people come to my office complaining that their parents run their lives, even after they are married. Often, a person that is 50 to 60 years old will complain that his 70 or 80 year old parents are driving him up the wall. When I ask him why he doesn't tell his parents how he feels, he generally says, "I can't talk that way to my parents; I would not want to hurt my Mother's feelings;" or "I just couldn't hurt my father's feelings that way."

As you remember, in earlier chapters, I explained to you that people choose their own feelings, so you must say what you think. People do not understand, until you tell them what you think. They can't see inside your mind. They cannot tell what you are thinking, so you must tell them.

Generally, the older a person gets, the smarter and the more cunning he becomes. If you are allowing your parents to run your life and you are an adult, it is probably because they are smarter at maneuvering people than you are. And, generally, the one motive they have in mind is to try to help you, because parents love their children. It makes no difference if they know how to show it or not. Parents love their children. So, when you look at your parents, look beyond the surface. See the real person, the father or mother that is doing what he or she thinks is right. I haven't met a person yet that has done something for any other reason. The person simply thinks he is right. So, the next time that one of your parents gets his feelings hurt because of something you do or say, that is his problem.

The best way to tell your parents "how the cow ate the cabbage" is to say to them, "Look, I think you are the best parents in the world. I love you dearly. I think you are the greatest." (That's the cookie.) "Now, get off my back." (That's the punch.) What you have done is, you have reassured them that you love them very much. You have told them they are the greatest, and then you have followed up and told them what you think about what they are doing. It's not a matter of believing your words yourself. It's a matter of manipulating the person, so he experiences a "feel-good" while you are giving your opinion.

The reverse is also true. As you know, as long as you believe he loves you and likes you and cares for you deeply, you will listen to what he has to say. Now, you can see how to throw the bear the cookie and hit him in the mouth without his ever knowing he was hit. So, if you tell someone that you like and respect him, but you don't particularly like the way he acts, you will get a lot further than you would if you verbally attacked that person with only negatives. As long as you don't attack someone personally, you can say what you want to say and they will choose to feel o.k.

The same procedure works in reverse when dealing with children. You must let them know that you love them dearly. It makes no difference if you understand or agree with them. You love them dearly and you are going to give them your opinion.

If you will develop this next little technique, I think you will find that you can get along with almost anyone. You might say to a person, "I may not understand how you think and it's not important that I agree with you, but tell me how you think. And, you may not understand or agree with me and that is all right, too. Let me tell you how I think." You will be amazed at the "feel-goods" this technique can produce.

Just remember: No one can read another's mind. You MUST say what you think and encourage others to do the same.

CHAPTER 9

TO DRINK OR NOT TO DRINK

Now, I will explain how to give up "Old Crow" and live a long, happy, and very healthy life. I have never met you, but, if you are an "Indulger of the Spirits," I can tell you why you drink. When it gets down to the bottom line, you simply drink to relax. No one ever sat you down and explained to you that you can become relaxed without spending your good money on alcohol. Once your body is perfectly relaxed, you no longer have the desire for alcohol.

It is a shame that churches have condemned you for drinking. Those people simply do not understand the feelings that you were experiencing in your body. They said that you were a sinner. They called you a bum! As I stated in previous chapters, those negative statements made by society were commands to your Subconscious for you to continue to drink. Had they understood how to give good commands to help you, they would have.

In the program that I will outline, you will have the choice to drink or not to drink. If you choose not to drink, you will find that you no longer have the desire to spend your good money for alcohol.

Let us start by taking a good look at liquor commercials. As I said in the chapter on smoking, almost all of the ads show some kind of connection to relaxation, having fun, or sexual connotations. It is impossible for cigarettes or alcohol to relax you, but the advertisements certainly do show people relaxing and having fun, while drinking and/or smoking.

When you have a drink, the alcohol enters into the

bloodstream and eventually travels to your brain. Once it is there, it breaks down the brain's ability to function normally. It changes the chemical structure of the brain cells and causes a variance in electrical charges that take place in the brain. So, if you are sitting there with a "numb" brain, chances are that you are not going to put as many negative thoughts into your Subconscious. Whenever you eliminate the negative input, the Subconscious takes care of you and gives you a "feel-good." If you put too much alcohol in the brain, you will become irrational and you might say or do anything.

You were not taught about the Subconscious. You may have drawn the conclusion that you enjoyed drinking. No, you enjoyed the "feel-good" that the Subconscious gave you from the lack of negative input.

The following is the program that you are to follow. YOU MUST DO EXACTLY AS I SAY! When you do, the desire for the alcohol will leave your body.

If you are sitting there reading this book and you are having a drink, simply finish your drink. Say the words, "This drink is the last drink of alcohol that I am going to drink, and it is the last drink that I am going to use to alter my brainwaves." GO AHEAD AND FINISH YOUR DRINK! DO NOT CONTINUE TO READ THIS CHAPTER UNTIL YOU HAVE FINISHED YOUR DRINK! Finished? O.K. Now, set the empty container out of sight.

Before you continue to read this chapter, take all of your alcohol and put it in a box or carton and seal it up! Get all of the alcohol out of the refrigerator or pantry and pack it away also. DO IT NOW! DO IT RIGHT NOW! Have you done it? You must do as I say, now. NOW is the only moment in your life, so do it NOW!

Good! NOW that you no longer drink, repeat in your

mind that you have finally given up drinking, and that it feels good now that you do not drink. Read the following and then, with your eyes closed, you are to repeat it in your mind several times:

"I am now a changed person.

I am now a very relaxed person.

I am now a good person and I see only good in my life.

I control my life and I control my body.

I have no problems. I have only situations and those situations can be either dealt with or set aside."

Now, put yourself into a deep, relaxed state and give yourself a reason for all of those things in the past that you did not understand. It does not make any difference whether or not the reasons are logical; just explain to yourself WHY those negative things happened. If those negative things had to do with something that involved people, remember that people have not been trained to think. People have been trained to react. Every person that ever did something, did it because that person thought that he was right. Even though it may not have been right for you, he thought that he was right. Just as, each and every time that you have done something, you have thought that you were right also, or else, you would not have done it.

In the future, you may be reminded of alcohol. If this happens, simply think to yourself that you are a changed person and that you do not care for alcohol. If you experience the feeling that you used to think was a feeling of wanting a drink, understand that it was not a feeling for alcohol. Instead, it was a "feel-bad," as a result of your accidentally having a negative thought. If you were unaware of the negative thought, it was the Subconscious sending you an uncomfortable feeling, as a result of negative conditioning. Now that you are in charge of your own conditioning, condition yourself to be relaxed and confident, in all situations.

You no longer have a poor self-image. You are a great person. You are a wonderful person. You are an attractive person. You are an intelligent person. In other words, you are all of the good things. You are all of these good things, because you are NOW in charge of your life. No one can see inside your mind, so think what you like. But think only healthy thoughts.

Repeat the relaxing exercise once or twice a day. A good time to do this is right before you go off to sleep at night and right after you wake up in the morning. *Anytime* is a good time, and *all of the time* is the time to be relaxed!

People will try to get you to drink, and they will act hurt if you do not drink with them. Remember, "hurt" is a feeling and feelings are a choice. If they choose to be hurt, that is their problem. It is not yours. Now sit back and see what drinking has gotten them. What did drinking get you? You experienced the "feel-good" and then maybe the hangover. How about having a "feel-good" all the time? What is the old phrase, "Misery loves company"? Look at that poor person that is drinking. He doesn't know how to relax, but now you do! You could tell him where to get a copy of this book, but, better yet, go out and buy him a copy and save his life! Show him how he can stay happy and healthy. Do not loan him your copy. Let him have his own.

Remember, because of what you say and what you think, you are now changed! You must repeat these words out loud, to your friends, and in your mind: "I am changed now. I do not drink. I feel fantastic as a non-drinker. I am relaxed, not drinking. I am a good person. I am a confident person. I am a happy person." When you do this, the Subconscious will make the words come true.

YOU DO NOT DRINK!
CONGRATULATIONS, YOU WONDERFUL PERSON, YOU!

P.S. If you have been successful in quitting drinking and are active with another program, continue with the program that works for you. This chapter is meant for those who have not been able to quit drinking by any means.

COMMENTS FROM CLIENTS

Tom Ray has introduced me to the concept of positive thinking, and it really works. At first, I thought very little of myself and I didn't believe that I could kick my drinking problem, but Tom said that he would stick with me for as long as it took and he did. As a matter of fact, even longer than was actually necessary, and I might add that it was at no extra cost to me.

Now I take an occasional drink because I want to and not because I feel that I have to and it is 98% social drinking with friends. For this I am very grateful to Tom. God Bless You, Tom, and Thank You!

* * *

I am 27 years old. I am married to an accountant. We have two young children. I am an alcoholic who no longer drinks.

I began drinking when I was 17 because it was daring to do something illegal and, according to my religious training, forbidden. I immediately liked the effect alcohol had on me, and drank whenever it was available to me. I got married shortly after my 18th birthday and drank very little for the next 3 years. I worked as a legal secretary and was considered a good one.

Then my husband joined the service and my life changed drastically. During the early months of his Army career, he was stationed away from me and I was on my own for what was actually the first time in my life. I could not stand the loneliness. I was very insecure and frightened. So, rather than go home to an empty apartment, I would go to a bar. This became a habit. A few months later, I joined my husband in Germany. During our separation, he had also spent a great deal of his time in bars, so it seemed only natural that we should continue drinking regularly together. Our marriage began deteriorating almost immediately and this gave me even more 'reason' to drink. After 5 years of marriage, we were divorced. I don't feel that alcohol caused the breakup of this marriage, but it certainly played a big part in it.

I stayed in Germany after the divorce. I had a good secretarial job there and many friends. My entire social life consisted of going to the bar at the Officers' Club, and this was where I met my present husband. We were married about a year after my divorce was granted, and returned to the U.S. My present husband was a heavy drinker when I met him and I can't recall a day during our courtship and first year and a half of marriage that we weren't drinking. But it didn't seem to affect him the way it did me.

I had been in several automobile accidents-all my fault-was having frequent blackouts and anxiety attacks. I was nearly always late for work, frequently absent, and was finally advised to take a few weeks off and rest by a doctor who didn't know I was an alcoholic. During that time, I was involved in another automobile accident, more serious than any before, and finally had to admit to myself that I had a drinking problem.

I was hospitalized for 30 days in an alcoholism treatment program. Within one month of my release, I was drinking again. I was seeing a psychiatrist, but quit because it interfered with my drinking. I got another job and was fired within 6 weeks for absenteeism. I can't remember how many times I have been in and out of the Alcoholics Anonymous Program. Nothing worked for me. My marriage was falling apart. My children were neglected. I couldn't hold a job. I had attempted suicide twice. My husband's job required him to travel a great deal and he didn't dare leave me alone because he never knew what I might do, or whether the children would be taken care of.

I was desperate for help when I decided to try hypnosis and called Tom Ray. With his help, I turned my life around. I have not had a drink since my first session. I have not had the desire to drink, even when I'm around other people who are drinking. I will soon have my real estate license and am looking forward to my new career. My husband has drastically curtailed his drinking, and our marriage is better than ever before. Our children are so much happier and more secure. I look better, feel better, have more energy and self-confidence, and am happier than I have ever been in my life.

I recommend hypnosis and Tom Ray to everyone!

* * *

CHAPTER 10
FAT IS NOT FOREVER

So, you want to lose weight! Overweight is probably the biggest problem that the people of America have today, no pun intended. The only reason people are overweight is because of the way they think, much more so than the way they eat. It is my belief that when a person says, "I am fat, I am fat. Oh, I hate being fat," he is just reinforcing the fact that he is fat and, therefore, he stays that way. Remember that the Subconscious Mind gives you what you ask for. Since it gives you what you ask for, you must say to yourself immediately, "I am thin. I act like a thin person. I walk like a thin person. I talk like a thin person, and I am getting thinner each day." Remember, this process is mechanical. You must mechanically say the words.

It is true that all the negative thinking that a person has done has simply caused a negative body response or a "feel-bad" and he then eats to try to feel good. If you are overweight, you have been told a jillion times that you cannot cope with life; you cannot cope with problems. These are negative commands from others and you simply must reject these commands by letting the words roll off like water off a duck's back.

I am saying that you simply have not chosen to cope with situations in the past, but because you have changed your way of thinking, you are now a positive person and you do cope with situations in your life or you ignore the situations. It is o.k. to ignore any situation. It is simply your choice. In fact, you no longer have problems; you only have situations. You know you choose your own thinking; you make your own decisions; and now you will simply choose to be thin. All you have to do is physically say the words, mentally think the words, and the Subconscious Mind becomes programmed in the positive.

If you say to yourself, "I cannot think that way and I will not think that way," that is o.k. with me. I want you to be what you want, and if you want to say, "I can't lose weight. I can't stay on a diet," that is your choice.

I would like for you to start noticing what other people eat. You will notice that the majority of the thin, slim people eat very little, and the majority of the heavy people eat as though it was their last meal. So, obviously, there is no such thing as a diet. There are different eating styles. As far as the overweight person is concerned, "diet" is a negative word. So, simply put in the place of the word, "diet," the words, "eating habits" or "eating style."

You are simply going to change your eating habits and thinking habits. One of the biggest mistakes that an overweight person will make is to say, "When I lose this weight, I will be a very, very happy person," and "Diets make me miserable." Now, tell me, how in the world can a person expect to stay on a diet or change his eating habits and be so miserable. I would not recommend that type of thinking to anyone.

What I recommend is simply being happy now. Be happy now, getting thinner each day. Be happy now, with a different way of eating. If you happen to say to yourself, "Well, I like all those fattening foods," I would say to you, "If you control your feelings, which you do, and if you control your likes and dislikes, which you do, you can simply choose not to like all those fattening foods. It is that simple." If you use the words, "but, what about," and "I can't," that is also your choice. I am telling you that the word, "but" should not exist in your vocabulary. "Butt" exists somewhere on your backside and is sometimes used in reference to cigarettes and cigars. Otherwise, "but" does not exist for you, now that you have changed.

The past does not exist. The future does not exist. The only thing that does exist is this moment. And when THAT moment is gone, we are in THIS moment. We are only in the NOW time frame, and if you have the strength to pass up certain foods NOW, you have the strength to pass up food at any time, even on Thanksgiving Day. So, by using this purely mechanical way of thinking, you lose weight and lose it very easily.

If you are having marriage problems, your marriage problems have absolutely nothing to do with the way you eat. If you are having financial problems, your financial problems have nothing to do with the way you eat, unless you do not have the money to buy food. If you are having problems of any kind, they have nothing to do with the way you eat.

How many times have you heard someone say, "This is not a good time to go on a diet"? Anytime is a good time to change the way you eat, unless it is your last meal. And if it is your last meal, obviously you were taught to do something you enjoy, so have that famous last meal. If you have not been sentenced and you are overweight, you might be sentencing yourself. I can think of a lot more interesting things I would like to do last, rather than eat.

Eating is designed for one thing and that is to replenish the body chemicals. Other than that, why eat? You have been trained that eating is a pleasurable thing to do. Go stand in front of the mirror and look at yourself. Now, tell me how pleasurable it has been. I am sure that you can understand that excess of any kind is not good.

It is amazing that in this world of ours, people spend millions and billions of dollars to lose weight, when all they have to do is choose a different way of thinking and eating. Why should anyone have trouble choosing a positive way of thinking? It is because he was trained to think negatively, as a result of his family, the school system, the community, and the religious structure. The only reason for this is that the ones doing the training thought they were doing it the right way.

Unfortunately, much of what they taught you was untrue, backward, illogical, irrational and incorrect. To give you a prime example: A preacher is standing in the pulpit, preaching the sermon. He thinks he is helping the people who came to his service, and he makes a comment of "How difficult it is to stay on the straight and narrow in this world today, and how easy it is to sin." So, when a person is walking along the straight and narrow and falls by the wayside, the Subconscious says, "Well, heavens. It's easy to sin. It is difficult to stay on the straight and narrow." What that preacher should have said is that it is easy to stay on the straight and narrow, and it is difficult to sin. Then, when a person goes out and gets into trouble, he will likely say, "I am going back to the straight and narrow where it is easy."

So now, you will simply choose to say the mechanical words and lose the weight, because you have changed your way of thinking. Use the relaxing exercise once or twice a day. Concentrate on a good self-image: how wonderful, attractive and intelligent you are. Give yourself the following commands:

I am a 100% healthy person.

I am calm and relaxed.
I am strong and confident.
I am thin, getting thinner.
Nothing bothers me.
I am a happy person.
I choose my feelings and I choose only happy feelings.
Over-eating is purely a waste of time.
I am not constantly hungry anymore.
I eat only to replenish my body chemicals."

You are in charge of your own conditioning now. You are a relaxed, confident, THIN person. It is EASY!

COMMENTS FROM CLIENTS

I have not only lost weight, but also have enjoyed every minute losing it. I am a very happy person. I have just experienced something I did not think I could. One of my experiences is that I can control my emotions. I was a very hot-tempered person. I would let any and every little thing worry me; now I do not allow myself to get upset.

* * *

For the first time in my dieting years, I feel good. I was a compulsive eater, which I'm not anymore. It amazes me that I can go shopping and bypass the forbidden foods. When I'm eating in a restaurant, I choose to eat the proper foods, no matter what anybody else is eating. Since I've been in hypnosis, my whole personal outlook has improved.

* * *

I definitely feel I have benefited from your sessions. In addition to losing weight and inches, I feel differently about dieting than I did in the past. Previously, I was always planning all the goodies I would eat when the diet was over. This time, I feel this is a permanent change in the way I want to eat. I don't think of myself as being on a diet. I choose to eat the way I do. I also have changed the way I think and feel about life in general. I think positively! I'm calmer at work and at home now.

* * *

You've helped me more than I ever could have imagined. I've lost 20 pounds, and I've gained back my self-confidence and drive.

For the first time in my life, I feel good and positive about every day. Your patience, thoughtfulness, and insight is uncanny and I'm forever grateful.

* * *

The world and other people used to handle my life; whatever was, was. I stayed nervous and keyed up, always trying to please everyone at all times. Also I was very much overweight and smoked, on top of that. My body was going down the drain.

Since I have been to Tom Ray, my whole life has changed. It's like walking into another world. I control Me now---no one else, not even the world.

I am more relaxed than I have been for 3 years. It's fantastic. I am losing weight and enjoying my life in the fullest. I am me.

* * *

NOTES

CHAPTER 11
ASTHMA BEGONE

Asthma is purely psychosomatic. A case in point follows. A 14 year old boy was brought to me because he was suffering from a severe case of asthma and also had a terrible-looking rash all over his body. After talking with the boy for a while and then with his mother, it was determined that the asthma started when he was about 4 years old. The rash had also developed at that time and had never left his body since, in spite of repeated visits to different dermatologists and allergists.

What happened? The family had been visiting relatives, and for some reason, the young boy became ill while having breakfast. From that day forward, he had trouble with his breathing. The doctors concluded that he had asthma. After many tests, the doctors told the parents that their son was allergic to everything, from grass to dust, many kinds of foods, and pets of all kinds.

I age-regressed the boy back through the years to determine what had caused him to develop the asthma and the allergies. I discovered that it was not the food he ate that caused the asthma and the allergies. Rather, it was his reaction to the hysterical attitude around him, created by his parents, because he had gotten sick while eating. His sickness caused the parents and relatives, who were possibly over-protective of the child, to become hysterical. The young boy became frightened, as a result of this hysterical reaction of the adults around him. Because the boy threw up his breakfast, his Subconscious Mind assumed that he was allergic to certain foods. The procedure continued to compound itself. From that day on, he had severe asthma, along with a rash over his entire body.

While he was in that super-relaxed state in my office, he rationalized his fears and put the wheels in motion for his Subconscious to allow him to be free from any uncomfortable feelings. I saw the boy on two consecutive days and again, a week later. On that third visit, he pulled up his shirt to show me his chest, which was free of rash for the first time in ten years! He related that in the last week, he had been able to eat anything he wanted and now had a pet bird and a pet dog! All this in one short week's time! The asthma also was gone. This was not a miracle. It was purely mechanical.

If you have a child that has asthma, teach him self-hypnosis, using the techniques as described in this book. If he is too young to teach self-hypnosis to, follow my instructions at the end of this chapter. Continue to read this entire chapter.

While in hypnosis, the child is to explain to himself that the reason for the asthma is no longer important; that he was born to be perfectly healthy; and that he is always 100% healthy. If he has any dermatitis or rash in connection with the asthma, he is to explain to himself that he is no longer allergic to anything and that the rash has gone away. This is very important. What happens in the conversation is that the Subconscious tries to fulfill these suggestions. He is to emphasize the fact that he is 100% relaxed, 100% healthy, and that absolutely nothing bothers him. All this is to be stated in the present tense, in the NOW.

There are millions and millions of people in the world today that are suffering from allergies, asthma and other forms of diseases that are purely psychosomatic, with no apparent cause. What happens is, the Subconscious gets a negative message. It produces an uncomfortable feeling and then, panic runs through the body. The body produces the feeling. The feeling is designed to warn the individual that something is wrong.

To give you a prime example, a lady walked into my office and said, "If there is one person in the room that has a cold, you can bet I am going to catch it!" And, sure enough, you could have someone in the room fake a cold, and this lady would come down with all the symptoms! Listen to the words some people were trained to use. How does a person catch a cold? Does she use a catcher's mitt? Does she catch it with her bare hands? Sounds a little ridiculous, doesn't it?

Each and every person that I have seen in my office with a complaint about his health, has been the result of thinking backwards, or negatively. Situations cannot upset people. People choose to be upset. It is unfortunate that people were trained to think in a backwards fashion. People were trained to think that if they did not feel good, they must be sick; rather than thinking constantly that they do feel good and there is no possibility of getting sick. How often have you said, "I don't have time to be sick," and then found yourself soon feeling better? How many people do you know that say they just don't have the time to get sick? How many people do you know that say they just do not allow themselves to become sick? If you think about it, those are probably the very people who seldom get sick and are always the picture of health.

This is very similar to the situation where two people are in the hospital and the one says, "Doctor, I have nothing left to live for." He dies, because he just gives up. The other person lives to enjoy those things he has to do and those places he has to go. His chance of returning to perfect health is greatly increased, because he has commanded his body to be that way.

If you have asthma or allergies or you have a child with asthma or allergies, follow the suggestions I have put forth in this chapter. Eliminate the negatives from your life. Be 100% healthy and happy.

As I promised, these are the instructions for a very young child with asthma. First of all, provide the child with a calm, relaxed environment. Give him or her all the commands verbally, that I mentioned earlier, as if you were giving the child commands for self-hypnosis.

Give the child the following commands in the waking state and also whisper them to the child when he or she is asleep. Make sure the child is sound asleep and then whisper the following: "Stay asleep. This is Mom (or Dad) talking. Stay asleep. I want to talk to you. You are a good child and I love you very much. You are a good child. You are a very relaxed child. You are a calm and happy child. You are safe and protected. Your breathing is always relaxed. You are a very healthy child, a relaxed and happy child. You are a strong and beautiful child. You are a wonderful, happy child. Whatever bothered you in the past is not important. You are happy and healthy now. You are always happy and healthy. Your parents and family always love you." You notice these statements are all positives in the present tense, as if they had already happened. This is very important. Do these things as I have said and you will soon be living with a healthy child, instead of a sick one.

COMMENTS FROM A CLIENT

For quite a number of years, I had allergic symptoms with increasing severity and frequent sinus headaches. About six years ago, I started going to an Allergy Clinic. The treatment would help me temporarily, but I had stopped using cosmetics and deodorants almost completely because of allergy symptoms.

Last August, I heard on the radio of Tom Ray's work with hypnotism for allergies, nervousness, and other disorders. At any rate, I decided to try hypnotism, largely because of my allergies and the fact that my memory had become impaired, following my husband's sudden death early in September of this year.

In the course of the hypnosis consultations, Tom Ray assured me that I did not have allergies, because allergies are psychosomatic conditions (or symptoms). Soon the usual symptoms of itching skin and eyes and stuffy head became much less noticeable, in fact, soon non-existent. Also, as he had suggested, I viewed all of the unhappiness of the recent past in a much less painful light. This has made those months following my husband's death seem much less traumatic. In fact, I remember mostly the happy times he and I had.

I would recommend hypnosis for anyone suffering from the loss of a loved one. The improvement in my memory has been phenomenal and is still increasing, and allergy symptoms have been much less troublesome. Hypnosis has served me very well.

Tom Ray may use any or all of these statements in any manner desired, as I know that it would be only for the good of humanity.

* * *

NOTES

CHAPTER 12

HELP CURE CANCER WITH WORDS AND THOUGHTS

The following paper was submitted to the San Antonio Chapter of the American Cancer Society in February, 1979 by Tom Ray.

* * *

So, you have cancer? Or you do not have cancer and you do not want to get cancer? It is my belief that 99% of all cancer and sickness is brought on by the way you think. Obviously, it is not your fault the way you think. You were trained to think the way you do. It is not your parents' fault nor your teachers' fault. It is no one's fault. It is just simply the fact that people get into a habit of thinking and talking negatively and do not realize they are doing so. Obviously, if they realized it and knew how to change, they would simply change. When I say to you that I think you can help cure cancer, by turning your thought processes around, don't waste your time telling me, "I did not think myself into this cancer. I did not ask for it."

In reality, your Subconscious is giving you cancer in an effort to warn you that something is wrong. Many of the thoughts and words you use are simply backwards. Your Subconscious records every word that you say and every thought that you think. You must use the proper word format to command the Subconscious in order to produce perfect health. Now, if you do what I say, exactly what I say, I think that you will find yourself cancer-free very soon.

First of all, you must continue to see your doctor. If you are going to a doctor and if he tells you that you only have five years to live, you tell him that in five years, you will be well. That, in fact, you will probably be well in six months. Then, you must explain to your Subconscious Mind how to do away with your cancer. After all, if you cut yourself accidentally, while peeling potatoes or chopping wood, your body heals itself. You do not use glue and cellophane tape to fix the cut. Surprisingly enough, your body will heal itself. So, you will simply command your Subconscious to heal your body from this disease. I know this sounds easy. It is very easy. You will realize that any first-grader can do what I am going to ask you to do.

The first step you must take is that of taking the responsibility for your own health. You must say to yourself, "I was responsible for my negative thinking. I am responsible for my own health. I have arrived at my condition only because of my past negative thinking and absolutely no one, absolutely nowhere, had anything to do with my cancer. I accidentally brought on the cancer and now I will eliminate the cancer."

The next step is to free yourself from all hate or negative thoughts about the past and future. Some people refuse to put down hate. It is easy to put down hate. Free yourself completely from all negative thoughts and all unpleasant experiences that have happened in the past. The way to do this is to command your Subconscious that the past is the past and that absolutely no one can affect the way you choose to feel or think. You choose your own feelings, and if you have had a running battle with a parent, a brother, a sister, a child, or a situation, you do not need it. You will simply say to yourself, "It makes no difference where I am, or what I am doing. I am perfectly relaxed and perfectly happy, because I choose my own feelings."

I will give you an example of a situation you might be in that you do not like. You are in a situation at work or at home or away from home and you hate it, or hate whom you are with. If you will remember, I just said you must do away with all hate. So, you will see the situation for what it is. You might not like the situation, but you are choosing to stay in the situation, because of certain obligations or for financial reasons. It would be foolish to stay in the situation and choose to be uncomfortable, because you know that you have accepted the situation. You cannot stand there and tell me that you have to stay in any situation. You could get up off your backside and move. And, if you cannot get up and move, ask someone to move you. If you have tried all avenues to change the conditions, and they don't change, then move. Someone will take you in. You can bet on it.

Many people say, "Daddy, Aunt Sarah, and Uncle Willie had cancer, and I will probably get it too. It runs in my family." It is my belief that cancer is not hereditary. The way you think is the closest thing to being hereditary that I know of, because your elders are the ones who taught you how to think. And, believe me, they thought they were helping you when they taught you how to think the way you do. When they gave you advice, they thought they were correct at the time. Generally, people do not intentionally give advice that they think is incorrect.

You have been conditioned up to today by the people and the world around you. It is now time for you to do your own conditioning, so that you can be perfectly healthy. Use your doctor's advice and take the medicine he prescribes, but take command of your body with your mind.

Now that you have decided that you and you alone, take the responsibility for your health, and the things that have happened to you in your past mean absolutely nothing, you are ready to eliminate the cancer.

You will take yourself into a deep, relaxed state (all this state consists of is deep relaxation) three times a day. While in your super-relaxed state, these are the exact words that you will use:

"The uncomfortable things that happened to me in the past mean absolutely nothing.

The reason they mean absolutely nothing, is they cannot be changed.

The reason the past is of no value, is that the past does not exist now.

I only remember the beautiful times of the past.

I am 100% healthy and free from the past.

I have eliminated all hate from my life: past, present, and future.

I fear nothing and I respect and stay away from things that appear to be dangerous.

I am a special person to myself.

I respect myself first.

I think only in the NOW and NOW is the only important time.

I am a totally relaxed person and nothing will change that.

I control my body functions; therefore, I command my body perfect health.

Those things that happened to me in the past that created uncomfortable feelings are no longer important.

I am free from the past.

I am totally relaxed.
I am a totally 100% healthy human being.
The cancer that was in my body is melting away like ice on a hot summer day."

At this point, use your imagination to see the cancer leave the body. Any process will do as long as it leaves. See the good cells destroy the bad, in any form that you wish to use.

Continue:
"I do the things I want to do and I do not do the things I do not want to do.
Most of all, I am comfortable with myself and the world around me.
I do my own thinking, and no one can see inside my mind.
I choose my own feelings; absolutely nothing bothers me.
I am 100% healthy and getting healthier every day.
I do not worry about the future; I plan only good things for the future.
I choose only happy and healthy feelings.
I am the person I choose to be."

The Subconscious understands the words, so say the words. If you don't like these words, use your own; but make sure your commands are in the present tense form---in the NOW. They must be positive and stated in the present tense.

Gentlemen, Ladies, and whoever you are, reading this book: I realize this is a very new way of thinking, but I do not think it is radical or I would not tell you this. I like to think I am a rational man and what I am saying to you is for the benefit of all human beings. You MUST take responsibility for the way you think. You MUST think only positive thoughts, so that your Subconscious will give you only positive feelings.

There are hundreds of thousands of different ways to visualize the cancer leaving your body. You accidentally allowed the cancer. Now you deliberately eliminate it. You must cause the cancer to be washed away, beaten away, melted away, pushed out, shoved out of your system or any other technique that you choose. But, you MUST actually see the cancer leaving your body. This is called imagination. The imagination process is actually suggestion. These suggestions are given to the Subconscious Mind and then these suggestions will be carried out by the Subconscious. As you understand from a previous example, if you put a dollar in your piggy bank, you are only going to get out a dollar. So, think the proper information to get proper results. If you have chosen to die, it is your choice. If you choose to live, it is very simple to do.

If you are dying because someone would be happy, someone would feel sorry for you, or you want to be a martyr, you are simply wasting your time. You don't have the power to make anyone, anywhere, feel a particular way. If you allow anyone, anywhere, to tell you how to live your life; again, you are wasting your time.

Your Maker, whoever you believe Him to be, designed you to be perfect and there is absolutely nothing wrong with being perfect. It makes no difference if your nose is in the center of your forehead and your right ear is on your left side and you look like you have been hit by a semi-truck, you are beautiful. You are a human being and from this day forward, command yourself that you are Number One.

The reason you are Number One? There is no one else

in the world like you, so you might as well take position Number One and be the person you choose to be, allowing yourself to be cancer-free forever.

*   *   *

This paper specifically mentions cancer. However, if you have poor health of another kind, or you do not want to have poor health, you may substitute the appropriate words in place of the word, *cancer*.

NOTES

CHAPTER 13

DO YOU HAVE KIDNEY PROBLEMS?

Earlier in this book, I mentioned that I would tell you about a very interesting case, concerning kidney disease. I like to take on one of every type of disease, so that I can prove that the mind can help make the body well. I remember back several years ago, that I wanted to see a young person that had kidney trouble. I was making a speech to a local women's group and I decided to put out the message that I was seeking a young person, between the ages of fifteen and thirty, who had kidney disease. I would take that young person, at no charge, and show him how to make his kidneys work normally.

    Several months went by, after I had put out the word and I had no takers. I had almost forgotten about that particular statement in that particular speech, when one day, in popped a lady who said that her mother had been at the women's club dinner the night I spoke of taking the kidney disease case, at no charge. She told me she had a son that was 21 years old and asked me if I could help him in any way. I told her that I was interested in working with her son, but only if she agreed to explain to the boy's doctor what I was doing, and that she continue to do what his doctor advised. Remember, I am not a member of the American Medical Association and I do not want to waste my time fighting with those guys. The young man was having to go to the hospital every other day to go through dialysis and that was the only thing that was keeping him alive. The dialysis filters the impurities from the blood. That is also the function of the kidneys.

When the young man came into the office and sat down, it was apparent that he was as jumpy as a cat on a hot tin roof. I started asking him questions right off the bat, just like I do everybody. I asked him what his problem was, even though I knew exactly why he was there. He told me that his kidneys did not work. He said the doctors told him that his kidneys were dead. I said to him that if his kidneys were dead, he would be dead. I said that the kidneys are not dead; they just are not functioning normally. I asked him why he didn't just crank up the kidneys and make them produce enough urine to filter the blood properly. Obviously, he said that would be great, but he did not know how to do it. I said, "I will simply show you how."

The young man had not produced a drop of urine for about two years. I taught him all the things you have read in this book, such as how the mind controls the body; how to be relaxed and confident in any and all situations; how to handle any situation; how to understand the human being, and why he does the things he does.

Just as I had expected, and sooner than I had expected, in about a week and a half, he was in the bathroom having his normal bowel movement and he passed a little urine. He was quite surprised when it happened, because that was the first urine that he said he had produced in two years. As time went by, I asked him to measure the urine that he produced, and it got better and better, even though he was still making his regular visits to the dialysis center at a local hospital.

I contacted his doctor and told him personally what was happening with his patient. Remember, it is the doctor's patient, not mine. The young man was my client. I am not a doctor. I am just the world's greatest mind control expert.

Do You Have Kidney Problems?

Sounds a little egotistical on my part, doesn't it? Well, I have to tell myself that, so that I will produce the best results. It's not important if you like it or not, because I don't care what you think. I care what I think. By the way, I do not control your thinking, and so why be concerned about something that I can't control. As far as that is concerned, I think that is good sound logic and the truth. I work only with truth.

Back to the doctor. When I told him what was happening, he sounded quite interested. I asked him to work with me on the project, and to this day, I have not heard a word from the doctor. Soon after I talked to the doctor, the boy quit coming to see me. I last heard that he was locked up and kept drugged at a local facility for the mentally unbalanced.

This young man was making great strides. I was teaching him to handle himself in this society, and he was mentally sound as a dollar, but my guess (and it is only a guess and you cannot sue me for guessing), the God Almighty American Dollar won out and the kid lost. Now, you tell me what is right. Use the System for your convenience. Do not be controlled by the System.

NOTES

CHAPTER 14

THE PROFESSIONAL ATHLETE

One of the things I really enjoyed, when I was at the Medical Center, was working with professional sports figures. In fact, if the person were making his primary living as a professional athlete, I would give him or her my services at no charge. If any person put his body and health on the line for the entertainment of the sports fan, regardless of how much money he or she made, I would show that person how to maximize his talents and still keep his body healthy.

If you are a president of a large company or a ditch digger or a secretary, you do not have to fight your way into work and then fight your way out. You do not have to abuse your body just to make a living. In some professional sports, there is no body abuse, but most sports are rough on the system. If I made a rule for one, it stood for all. That free time that I gave was on a space-available basis only. If I spoke to a team somewhere, there was no charge, except for my expenses.

Professional athletes are already proven champions and I enjoy associating with champions. The professional athlete has already proven that he is a capable, thinking, intelligent human being. It is always a pleasure to work with these people.

I have heard many a coach say that the professional athlete is a spoiled prima donna. After talking to many of these people on a one-to-one basis, I find them to be very good, concerned people with interests other than money or their own popularity. Of course, there are a few exceptions.

There was a time when I spent a lot of my time going

to the San Antonio Spurs professional basketball team practice sessions. I believe it was during the 1979-1980 season. I met the team's general manager at a Roast the city fathers gave for the team captain, Jimmy "The Snake," or "Captain Late," Silas. I don't know how Jimmy got the nickname, "The Snake," but it was easy to see how he got the name, "Captain Late." That is, if you ever saw him play. During the late seconds of the game, all you had to do was give the ball to Jimmy and he would save the game. He is one of the best one-on-one players I have ever seen.

At the Roast, I met Bob Bass, the Club's General Manager and explained to him that if he ever needed my services, that they would always be available. We discussed what I could do to keep individual members of the team motivated.

Some time went by before Bob called my office. He had a young player that he wanted me to make as tough as a "junk-yard dog." I worked with this young man and he went on to develop into one of the dominant players in the National Basketball Association. Not only were his stats good, but he would run over six freight trains without a second thought. This young man turned into one of the finest team players in the League---a real asset to any team.

Bob asked me several times to work with individual players, but to this day, he has never agreed that I did them any good. However, he kept asking me to talk with individual players, so he must have seen some good in my work.

Some of the players didn't mind the media knowing about their visits to my office, and others did. I can understand why some of those that came to see me did not want to explain to the media what they were up to.

Therefore, any information about the players' visits to me came from the players themselves, not from me. I knew firsthand what was going on, but what was printed in the papers was "hyped up" to make it sound like something it was not. This was not always the case with some of the sports writers. Some of them printed exactly what the players told them. Those that are often interviewed must select their words carefully. When it comes to the San Antonio Spurs, those guys cannot go to the bathroom without the media wanting to print it. I understand the media boys; they are trained primarily to sell papers, not to print the exact news.

Toward the end of the season that year, the Spurs management got a wild hair and decided to fire the head coach, Mr. Doug Moe. This seems to be the practice of the Spurs management: firing the coach. Don't ask me why. They just do it. Coach Doug Moe had lost four games in a row, which is not unusual in the National Basketball Association. Especially when the team plays 84 games in a season. Well, Doug looked up and was out of a job. Bob Bass took over the job as head coach and also retained his title as General Manager.

Doug Moe was more of an offense coach than a defense coach and the Spurs led the league in offense and trailed the league in defense. If you have ever studied sports, you know a good defense is mandatory for success. Doug did take the team further than most, just on a good offense. That's a feat that not too many coaches can boast about.

After Doug was fired and Bob was hired, a couple of games went by and the Spurs lost two more games. I had stayed in touch with Bob Bass during the season and I decided to ask him to let me talk to the team as a whole, rather than just one-on-one. He consented and he allowed me about thirty minutes on one day and about ten minutes the following day. When I got through with my two brief sessions, the Spurs actually played good defense. The next two games, one with Boston and the other with Philly, the Spurs played like a fantastic pro-basketball team. They lost those two games, but went on to win the next eight straight, which is very good in the NBA. There was only one problem...Bob never asked me back. I remember that year the Spurs did well enough to make the playoffs and the team captain, Jimmy Silas, asked me if I was going to Houston with them to start the first round. I told him that the management had not asked me to go. The Spurs lost in the first round.

In forty minutes, I gave the team direction. You must understand that not everybody was trained to have the strength of conviction that I have, or the ability to convey that conviction.

This is the world of specialization. It is impractical to expect every coach to have all the qualities to produce a consistent championship team. When you have this occur, you will have a coach that is an extraordinary man. When you have a toothache, you do not go to the foot doctor. Right behind the Spurs trainer and doctor should be Tom Ray. The team has the coach for the mechanics of the game; the assistant coach to support the coach in the game plan, and the trainer and the doctor to help out when a player gets hurt, but nothing to help keep the players mentally prepared. Many people say that is a job for the coach. The coach usually claims that is the job of the individual player, therefore, the player continues his backward thinking and continues not to know the difference. I say it is the job for me. One day, I will be on the Spurs coaching staff.

*Here I am, 20-odd years later and the Spurs have not hired me. It may be a surprise to many that I like to think I helped the Spurs get their NBA Championship in 1999. I think, as a result of a letter that I wrote to three different people, (those people will remain nameless) my suggestions helped get the Spurs over the hump. My effect on the Championship may have only been one-half of one-millionth of one percent. I think I should have been on the stage the night of the Championship ceremonies in San Antonio, when they introduced the players and coaches from the past. I believe I made a difference in that 1999 Championship. I will always believe I have to my credit one NBA Championship. The nice part about it is that I can think as I please! "Sports Illustrated" interviewed Bob Bass and asked about the Spurs' earlier days. He spoke of a hypnotist, gave no names, and indicated it did little good. Why, then, did he tell the local papers at the time that what I did for the team was very positive? Why did he tell me one day, "Stay out of the Spurs' locker room. I don't want you taking over my team"?

I really like Bob Bass. He just missed it or refused to acknowledge that I was good at what I did: teach. That's all. I just teach. I am not a basketball coach. I am just a simple teacher. Bob, I still like you, whether you like me or not.

By the way, Bob Bass is one of the smartest men in basketball. He has always had a job in pro-basketball, while most of the other guys come and go. When it is all said and done, there will be Bob Bass, the genius that he is, still working in professional sports.

NOTES

CHAPTER 15

HYPNOSIS IN OUR EVERYDAY LIVES

If the people of the world only understood that they constantly use their Subconscious Minds without realizing it, they would demand to know more about the subject. And once they understood it, they would demand that their children be taught the same information. One of the biggest drawbacks to hypnosis or, the *Science of the Subconscious*, is its history. In our society, people refused to accept little they could not prove or explain. Because of stage hypnosis and Hollywood hypnosis, people became very skeptical. Dracula does not exist, nor does the Fair Maiden. Along the same line, Hollywood hypnosis and stage hypnosis is only for selling tickets. People have been taught that they could possibly lose control of their minds, when hypnotized. People have been taught that they could wind up in a desert, wandering aimlessly. This is just not true. You might ask, "How did these stories get started?"

It worked like this. The stage hypnotist, before he arrived in a town, would send a news release to the local newspaper explaining how someone, somewhere, had been a "victim" of hypnosis. Then, when this hypnotist arrived in that town, people would pay to see a freak show. There is absolutely nothing wrong with a freak show, as long as you understand that it is just a show. I have been asked many times at a speech or lecture to perform stage hypnosis. But, that is simply not my game. Part of my job is to stamp out this type of misleading information.

In years gone by, hypnosis was used and not understood. Hypnosis was unexplainable and a tremendous number of so-called facts were established about the subject. There are three different schools of thought on how hypnosis should be applied. In one application, the hypnotist performs the hypnosis on the subject. In the other, the hypnotist teaches the hypnosis to the subject. The third way is my way: I teach the *Science of the Subconscious*. When one is performing hypnosis on the subject, a professional hypnotist can expect only about 25% good results. When teaching hypnosis, the subject can use his Subconscious power, after he leaves the office, within the limitations of hypnosis as it is generally understood. Unfortunately, too many of the so-called professional hypnotists do not fully understand the Subconscious. When using this type of procedure, one can expect the success rate to be about 35%. Then, there is the *Science of the Subconscious*. I show how to totally control the illogical Subconscious, for 100% results!

    I just returned from a family reunion, where an aunt of mine made the statement, "I do not believe in hypnosis and I do not believe that the mind has that kind of power." As a result, she is choosing to block off a very powerful part of her being. She is choosing to think negatively. She is choosing to have a closed mind. I cannot understand why any person in the world would openly say, "I choose to be negative," especially after learning of the possibilities of her own mind. And, then again, her negative approach is understandable. She was simply conditioned to think the way she thinks. I guarantee you, there are people out there choosing the negative and understanding that they are doing so, but, unfortunately, not knowing how to change.

    There are many forms of hypnosis that occur in our daily activities. Day-dreaming is a form of hypnosis. Driving down the road and not remembering that you drove through a small town is an example of having been, for a short time, in a light, hypnotic state. Your Conscious Mind was thinking about something else, but your Subconscious Mind kept you on the highway. If your Conscious Mind had drifted too far away from the highway, your Subconscious Mind may have followed and, as a result, there would have been the possibility of an accident. Hypnosis could be called, "very deep concentration or thought."

When you are reading a book and you block out the noises around you, that is a form of hypnotism. When you watch TV or a movie and you become engrossed in the story, that is a form of hypnotism. Taking a nap and not being quite asleep and not being quite awake, is a form of hypnotism.

You must be aware that your Subconscious Mind is with you 100% of the time, so when you allow your mind to wander, your Subconscious Mind tries to take care of you. Your Subconscious Mind is what keeps your heart beating and your lungs breathing. You can control both functions with your Subconscious Mind, because your Conscious Mind can direct the Subconscious.

I am calling now to the general public to demand that your children be taught the *Science of the Subconscious* and mind control. After I have finished this book, I am going to prepare a textbook that should be adopted by your schools. This text will teach your children mind control. But, until then, you must teach your children to think before acting. Do not wait for the school text. Get your children a copy of this book.

If you see a school text on hypnosis or the *Science of the Subconscious*, you can put away all fears about the teacher being able to hypnotize and the students being under her control. That is simply just not the case. Through a program that I call Positive Mind Power, your children can learn at a very young age to control their bodies and their minds themselves, rather than having all the negatives heaped upon them by our antiquated, backwards, negative system.

Our system that we have now, obviously, is better than anything we have ever had, and I am thankful that it is as good as it is. That is what they said about the Model T Ford: "Look how wonderful it is." It is good that we always like to change the system and make it better. I feel this is a healthy outlook. Some people are afraid of change and say, "Don't rock the boat. Don't change the system." If, with a positive attitude, we can turn that type of thinking around, we will gain ground much faster than we have gained ground in the past. I realize that new ideas should be proven before being fully implemented, but let's make an effort to be faster at proving new ideas and at eliminating out-of-date ideas. And, surprisingly enough, faster can be done with a relaxed approach. When I say out-of-date, I mean ideas that no longer apply. I know many long-distance runners that can run better when they are relaxed than when they are uptight. So, the more relaxed we are, the more efficient, faster, and skilled, we become.

If you are a young man or young lady reading this book, do not rely on your teachers and your parents to motivate you. The responsibility for your life is on your shoulders. You can motivate yourself with positive manipulation of the Subconscious. Tell yourself that you are super-great and that you have what it takes, and your Subconscious will produce that condition.

I was watching a movie recently about three young

astronauts who were stranded in the desert. Across the desert was a very high, rough, rugged mountain range. They decided to split up, so that at least one of them would, hopefully, make it back to home base. One went to the right, one went to the left, and one went toward the mountain range. I remember what the astronaut said when he saw that big mountain range. He said to himself. (actually, out loud, so the audience could hear it) "It's a piece of cake."

He was conditioning himself, so when he got to the mountain range, it would be very simple for him to go over those mountains. Had he told himself that it would be impossible, sure enough, it would have been impossible.

Bear in mind that the Subconscious is going to give you what you ask for, so do not depend on other people to condition you. Condition yourself. Do not wait for the world to be right so that you can be happy. Be happy first, so the things in your world are right. If they are not right, see the good side anyway. Protect yourself, but see the good side of life. It would be foolish to say, "When everything is o.k., I will be happy." You choose your own feelings, so be happy now and, amazingly enough, things will become better. If you say that things will not get better, you are simply commanding them to stay bad.

If you say that the world will not get better, you're not only putting negatives into the Subconscious, but you are attempting to predict the future. Nobody has been able to 100% accurately predict the future yet, and you are not likely to be the first.

You are responsible for your own happiness, regardless of the condition in which you live. Give yourself positive information about the way you are to feel; the world around you will change; and you will be surprised at the change. If you do not want to accept the world around you and you choose to be negative, at least, choose to be happy while you're being negative.

That reminds me of a recent client. He was an alcoholic and had heard one of my radio broadcasts. After listening to what I said on the air, he decided that he would be a happy drunk rather than an unhappy drunk! Well, that didn't work either, so he decided to be happy not drinking, and that was the answer. He now says that he sees the world in a totally different perspective. He is a healthy, happy, relaxed, successful non-drinker now. All because he decided that he was responsible for his own happiness. You can do it too!

CHAPTER 16
THE MEDIA

Now that you have become a thinker and are no longer just a reactor, you will also no longer be a victim of some of the advertising media's highly refined brainwashing techniques. Those in the advertising trade know full well that you were not trained to think; that you were simply conditioned to react; and they are taking advantage of that fact in almost every product promotion that they handle.

With my graduate level education in marketing and actual experience in the marketplace, plus my knowledge of the *Science of the Subconscious*, it is easy for me to see what I call unfair trade practices in many of the advertising promotions that bombard the public on a daily basis. There are a few companies that promote their products with truth and honesty, but I wonder just how few.

One way to protect yourself is to understand that the company's claims are usually exaggerated and biased. Double-checking and triple-checking might just save you some time and money.

You should be very cool and calculating when making a purchase of anything other than the proven products that you use. I am talking about changing product brand. I mean something so simple as changing your brand of coffee. Let's take a look at the following type advertisement. Consider the example of a frequently run television commercial for caffeine-free coffee. Scene: Mr. Joe Citizen is putting on a display of nervousness and irritability. (He is a paid actor and not a person in a real-life situation.) Then enters a well-known, recognizable actor that for many years played the role of the wonderful, helpful, family doctor. The famous actor turns to the so-called nervous and upset, Mr. Joe Citizen and comments about his case of the upsets. The nervous one claims that his doctor told him that the caffeine in his coffee was making him nervous. Without confirming or denying the statement, the famous, well-known, wonderful, lovable, highly-paid actor simply suggests that he should try "Sinko," the caffeine-free coffee. The next scene shows the same Mr. Joe Citizen, now as a calm, happy fun-loving person, claiming that he has switched to "Sinko" and now he feels so much better.

Because of the way we were conditioned not to think, the obvious conclusion might be that if we were nervous and upset, it might be the brand of coffee that we drink. The solution: Buy "Sinko," the caffeine-free coffee.

I will bet you my house, my car, my wife, and my children that if you bring me a person who believes that caffeine makes him nervous, within the space of one hour in my office, he will no longer believe and react to the caffeine in his coffee. My own lovely mother thinks that if she has a cola or a cup of coffee any later than 4:00 in the afternoon, she will not be able to sleep at night. Hogwash! However, if the so-called illogical Subconscious has recorded that message, then she truly will not sleep at night, after she drinks a cola or coffee.

Remember, the Subconscious does as it is told, without regard to logic. If you do not control your Subconscious, it will control you and sometimes you may not like the results you get.

Just a few nights ago, I was watching TV and, in one commercial, a lady was complaining about how tough her day was and that the days were getting tougher. The whole message was that when you have a tough day, just take this little pill and everything will be o.k. Now, you can see why many people today are strung out on drugs. They were told by the TV commercials that it is o.k. to take those pills, so that they will feel better.

The problem with the drug scene today is not the pusher, not the manufacturer, and not the grower. Instead, it is the conditioning of the poor human from the time he hits the ground at birth, until now. He is taught not to think. He is taught merely to react. He is asked to purchase products that have little or no redeeming value. He is asked to purchase products that have no worthwhile effect on his body. You, the general public, from every walk of life, are allowing this negative cycle to continue. You have tried to deal with the symptom and have totally overlooked the problem. The problem: "Teach the child what makes the mind and body work together. Teach him what is truth and what is not truth."

Let's go back to the lady that is having the tough day. Obviously, that is lousy perception on her part. I have never had a tough day and I don't intend ever to have a tough day! At one time, I worked from daylight to dark in the oil fields and I simply did not perceive of it as tough. Sure, there is such a thing as body fatigue, but if you condition yourself to be relaxed, while you push that barge and tote that bale, then you will experience less fatigue.

The human is trained to hit the couch at the end of the day or at the end of many hours of activity and say to himself, "Boy, I am beat." Well, that statement is nothing more than a command to the Subconscious to create more of a fatigue feeling. For better results, when you hit the couch at the end of the day, it would be more logical to say to yourself, "I am relaxed. I am calm. It was a good day and tomorrow is going to be an even better day." With these thoughts, the body relaxes and the body is then allowed to repair, so that you can continue to the next day as a very healthy person.

Do you wonder why they call a television set, the "Boob Tube"? Let's use television for fun and education, not just as a trash passer. Think about what you are exposed to on TV, radio, and in newspapers, magazines, etc. Think! You can say, " NO" to those lousy media commands.

CHAPTER 17

YOU HAVE BEEN BRAINWASHED

In this world of ours today, the system is constantly trying to brainwash you. Not only are you brainwashed by television, but you are brainwashed by your family, your neighbors, your teachers, and even by your preachers. How many preachers do you know who would turn to the bank robber, dope addict, or alcoholic, and say: "Come into the House of the Lord. You are a good person. Let me show you an easier way to be happy and healthy"? Generally, preachers have been known to say: "I know that you are a sinner, and so on and so forth." The Subconscious does not want to hear that it has done wrong, so the person stays away from the church. He was probably trained, as a child, to believe that he should go to church and that when he stays away, he is in for additional uncomfortable feelings.

You know now that no one can see inside your mind and no one can tell what you are thinking, so you are free to go to the church of your choice and do as you please. Remember, you will probably meet people that speak and act in a negative manner, even in church, but because you are changed, you are no longer affected by your environment. You are like me now; you affect your environment; and you affect it the way you choose...in a happy, healthy, logical, loving way.

Unless you are in charge of your Subconscious, you are brainwashed everywhere you go, even at home. The father might say, "You dummy, do it right." Then, when the child does something wrong, he reinforces the fact by saying, "I am a dummy. I am stupid." Then, he continues acting out the command. In essence, what the father is doing is confirming to the child that the child could not think or did not know how to think. So, the whole idea is to teach the child not to do it again, by giving him a positive, by confirming the fact that he is a smart child, and by saying, "You are a smart child. Next time, do it this way. You are very capable. You know the difference between right and wrong. You have proven in the past, on many occasions, that you are brilliant, so continue to do the right thing."

When was the last time you complimented one of your children or one of your friends for doing something right? If you only reward your children with negatives, they will get in the habit of seeking negative rewards and you will really have a problem on your hands.

Now that you know how the Subconscious Mind works, if you choose to be negative, it is simply your choice, no one else's. There is absolutely no way that you can make someone else happy and there is absolutely no way that you can make someone else mad. People choose their own feelings. So, if that is the case, do what you want to do, within the framework of the law. Of, if you choose not to go by the law, accept the consequences. You chose them.

If you think that you cannot say what you think, to another person, you are only fooling yourself. You can say the words and if the other person chooses to get upset, that is his problem. If you give the person a "positive" first and recognize him for being a human being and then tell him you don't like something, you will get more mileage than if you attack him personally. "I think you're a great person, and I respect you as a friend, but I do not like what you did. Please don't do it again." A person cannot argue with that approach, but if you just say, "I don't like what you did," he will generally react in a negative fashion, because he has been trained in a negative environment. He may think it is a personal attack, which it is not.

That is one of the big mistakes humans make today. People attack one another, rather than attacking what the other person did. All of you are good people. Some people continue to be very negative, primarily because they were brainwashed or trained to do so. They may not realize, however, that they are being negative.

Now that you understand how the Subconscious works, stop that brainwashing process and condition yourself the way you would like to be. I have never met a man yet, that did not want to be a good man. You are the way you think. If you are choosing to think negatively, you are not impressing anyone. Now, you know that people choose their own feelings. So, be positive and, at least, your friends may choose to be impressed. If they are impressed, o.k., and if they are not, that's o.k., too. You will have better luck dealing with people by using a positive approach than you will a negative one. The majority of people you will meet do not like negatives, even though they might be living examples of negative conditioning.

Now, you can take charge of your life and make yourself happy and healthy and successful, by simply thinking of yourself that way. Make the change this very moment. It is very simple. You relax yourself. Tell yourself that you are a positive person. When you say you are a positive person, that will take care of every situation you get into. You will automatically react like a positive person and you will find that it comes naturally. You will feel healthier, happier, and stronger. And, guess what? Others may like what they see. Maybe they will also choose to be positive.

Then you can say, "I was able to help someone else, but I helped myself first."

Now that you understand that you were simply taught to be the way that you are, that you were brainwashed or conditioned, it is your choice to be the type of person you choose to be. Now choose only the good things. Choose to be attractive, calm, relaxed, healthy, strong, confident, intelligent, and successful. There will be people that will never change, but that is of no concern of yours. If you choose to remain in their company, do not compromise your ideals and beliefs. Be the person YOU want to be, regardless!

CHAPTER 18

THE SUPER SALESMAN

So, you would like to be a Super Salesman. It is very simple. First, I would like to tell you about my selling experiences. My first real selling-learning experience came when I worked for a chemical company. These people knew how to teach selling. The management of all the other firms I had worked for knew nothing about teaching salesmanship.

Everybody seemed to be selling chemicals in those days, so I had competition everywhere I went. I learned the "hard sell" and, believe me, it works. I have heard people say that they just could not sell if they had to be pushy. Let's change the word, "pushy" and call it: "Do not accept "No" for an answer." If you are in the selling game and you do not like the hard sell, you had better change professions. The object of selling is to sell.

Why call on the customer, unless you expect to make a sale? Everyone is a buyer. From the beginning of our lives, in today's world, we were taught that it is fun to buy. So, you know that the person you are talking to was conditioned to enjoy buying.

Always ask for a much larger sale than you expect to get. You will be surprised when the buyer will take that larger order. Then you will really be ahead of your quota.

When your customer says, "No," restate your point in other words, just as though you did not hear the "No." If you do not get at least five "No's," you are not doing your job. If your customer asks a question about the product or service, as far as you are concerned, that is a "buy" sign. Tell yourself that if the customer says, "No," that's a "buy" sign. Tell yourself that the tougher the customer, the easier the sale. If the competition is mentioned by your customer, do not discuss the competition. Instead, restate a strong point of your product. Never debate the competition with your customer. This puts the customer in the selling game, of selling the competition. And, believe me, he is the man that has the power of the pen and if he loses the debate, he will probably not buy your product.

Success in selling is also in the numbers. The more people that you call on, the more chance you have of making a sale. If you sit at home on your backside or spend most of your time having coffee, you will not sell your product. Start your day as early as possible. This gives you more time to make more calls. Remember the numbers. No calls...no sales!

If you are going out of your shop to make the call and it is a cold call, do not wait for your customer for more than ten minutes. While you are waiting to see the customer, you could be selling someone else. Qualify your buyer. If he or she is not the buyer, do not waste your time or your sales pitch. If they do not have the power of the pen, do not show your product.

Almost every Super Salesperson has some form of a daily plan: a call sheet. You plan your calls and after each call, you record all the pertinent facts about the call. Record the buyer's name, age, type of person, noticeable traits, likes and dislikes, work schedule, family, kids; anything that could be mentioned on your next visit. He will think you are truly interested. Act sincere. If there is to be no next visit, that's all right. Everyone likes to talk about himself.

If your customer needs a son, play the role of a son. If

your customer needs a mother or a father, play the role. If your customer needs a friend, play the role of a friend. You do get the picture, don't you?

When the customer gets to talking too much about himself, you must guide him back to the purpose of your being there. If he tells you that he does not buy your type of product, that means he may not have any of your type product on hand. Therefore, in your mind, he needs some. If he has too much of the type of product that you are selling, that means he is a buyer and you will sell him even more.

If you use an order pad, have it out in plain sight. You are simply letting him know that you are there to do business and you expect to make a sale. After he has said, "Yes," write it down. Once you write it down, he may think that he is committed. After you have the order written and it looks like you are finished, give him the pad and pen. Tell him to "Sign right here." Do not ASK him to sign the order. TELL him to sign it, such as, "Sign right here, sir." "Would you?" is a question and this leaves you open to get a "No."

After you have the signed order and you are getting ready to leave, tell him you are going to send him some of your new product to try. Then, add it to the order. Do not ask him if you can send some of the new product to try; tell him you are going to send it. If he does not say, "No," you have added to the size of the order.

Always have a promotion. Whether you have a promotion or not, tell the buyer that you are having a big promotion. If it is around Christmas, you are having a Christmas Promotion. If it has just rained, you are having a Rainy Day Sale. If it is close to Washington's Birthday, you are having a Washington's Birthday Sale. If it is close to Groundhog Day, you are having a Groundhog Day Sale. If there is a dead dog on his front lawn, you are having a Dead Dog Sale. Get the picture?

If you have used every trick in your bag and the customer does not buy, tell yourself, as you walk out the door, that your odds are getting better. If you normally write one sale out of four, that means that one of the next three will buy. If the second customer of the day does not buy, you tell yourself that your odds are getting better because one of the next two will buy for certain. The game of selling is primarily the game you play with yourself. You are simply going to set the scene and sit back and watch the customer react. Remember, he was trained to react, not to think.

There are thousands of little techniques that you can use in the selling game. Many of the above techniques can be applied to any type of selling. When you use just a few of the above-mentioned techniques, plus the mental suggestions to yourself about how good you are at selling, then you become a Super Salesman.

The most important thing that you must do in the selling game is to always be honest about your product. Never, I say, never, misrepresent your product or service. If you do, you will soon be out of the selling business. Always do what you say you are going to do. Always. Selling is one of the easiest, one of the most exciting, and profitable businesses you can be in. Enjoy it!

CHAPTER 19

OPINION VS. EMOTION

Opinion has nothing to do with emotion. Unfortunately, those that taught us simply did not know. I wonder where it all got started.

"I don't like what they did and it makes me mad." If you have ever heard phrases like this, and I know you have, it is a result of one of the biggest frauds perpetrated on mankind, ever.

Unfortunately, you were taught that your own opinion about other peoples' actions or world conditions had a direct effect on your emotions. You were taught they had a direct effect on whether you were mad, happy, etc.

Think about it for a moment. What does the flat tire on your car have to do with the emotional condition of your body? Nothing. It is o.k. not to like a situation, but it is not o.k. to get mad, angry, upset, nervous, and so forth.

For example: "I cannot stand what the government is doing to all of us. It makes us all so nervous." I ask you, what do the boys in Washington and what they are doing with our money have to do with my body here in Texas? Nothing. Also, the statement is a command for everybody to be nervous. "All of us" included you. Yes, you, the person reading this book. If you do not become a good listener and say, "No" to negative commands, you become a victim of those commands.

So, when they say, "us, we, our," you are included. I refuse to let the world put garbage on me like that. I can say, "No" in my mind and no one will ever know.

"I just hate those people. It makes me so upset." First

of all, hate is an extremely unhealthy opinion. You probably thought hate was an emotion. Why would someone choose to hate, once he realized its dangerous consequences on the body? Hate is the most heinous of all opinions. Hate is so severe, the mind will have you do strange things that will probably get you in deep trouble, both legally and psychologically.

Hate is an opinion. Opinions, like emotions, are a choice. It seems to me that hate is a pretty lousy choice.

By the way, how another person lives, walks, talks, eats, sleeps has nothing to do with my body. It is o.k. not to like what someone else does, as long as he stays within the confines of the law, but it has nothing to do with my body.

So, if you hear someone say, "We all just hate those people and it makes me so sick," if you do not say, "No" to that type of a negative command, you automatically agree. The absence of "No" is "Yes." That means you become affected by any old conditioning, to respond with a "feel-bad."

The Subconscious Mind is designed to protect us. When hate takes place as an opinion, we were taught to have a "feel-bad." The Subconscious Mind will cause the body to do strange things in order to get rid of the "feel-bad." The illogical Subconscious Mind was taught to have a "feel-bad" with a negative opinion, even though opinions have nothing to do with emotion.

Now you know why there are wars, killings, beatings and violence of all kinds. The mind is trying to get rid of the "feel-bad" created by an opinion called hate.

CHAPTER 20

HERE'S JOHNNY...THE 'TONIGHT SHOW' THAT ALMOST WAS

I have been patient. I have waited for about twenty years to get on Johnny Carson's "Tonight Show." I hope that I can get on the "Tonight Show" before Johnny Carson decides to hang it up.

Maybe I should start from the beginning. Way back in October of 1965, I had gone to New York City to train to be a medical supply salesman. I was just out of the U.S. Air Force and I had recently found some Spanish silver on Padre Island, off the Texas Gulf Coast, while on a treasure hunting expedition. I decided to take the silver reales with me to New York and use them as an entree to get on the "Tonight Show" with Johnny Carson. I was just a young man from a small town and I thought the story about the Spanish treasure would be interesting to other people. I was really naive! If Mr. Carson agreed, I was going to show him and his young sons the thrill of finding Spanish treasure on Padre Island. At that time, when the conditions were right, a person could walk along the beach, like my friends and I did and just pick up 400 year old Spanish coins, as easily as picking up seashells.

There I was, in the big city and I was going to figure out a way to talk to Johnny Carson! If you have ever tried to get to a big celebrity like Johnny Carson, you know that unless you have the inside track, it is not easy to do. Maybe there is an easy way, but I do not know it. I went to the building where the "Tonight Show" was taped, and started asking where I could find Johnny's secretary. I made the question sound as though I was not interested in seeing Johnny Carson, just his secretary. I walked up to a security guard and asked where I could find Johnny Carson's secretary. I did not even know her name, and the guard said, "You mean Jeannie Pryor?" I said, "Yes." Now I had a name, and off down the hall I went!

I made it up to the next floor and I was stopped by another security guard who asked me where I was going. I played it cool and said, "I'm looking for Jeannie Pryor, you know, Johnny's secretary." He sent me down the hall and up a few more stairs. By this time, I was doing great! I had gotten past two checkpoints and I was on my way to a personal visit with Johnny Carson. There I was with a briefcase full of Spanish treasure and on my way to stardom! My stardom seemed to collapse when I next talked to a lady that claimed to be Jeannie Pryor's secretary. I had not planned for her to have her own guard and checkpoint. I was stopped cold in my tracks and told to go home and write to one of their talent scouts.

I was to be in New York for only a few days and being the type that doesn't give up, I hired a secretarial service to type a letter to Johnny. I figured that with a little ingenuity and some guts, I would meet Mr. Johnny Carson, face to face. I made up a package with the letter and pictures of the old Spanish silver. If I did not get to see Johnny Carson, I would mail the package to him while I was there in New York City.

With a little amateur investigating, I learned that Mr. Carson kept his limo and driver parked out on the front street. All I had to do was wait until his show was over and when he came out to get into his car, I would meet him, talk with him, and tell him my story, along with giving him the package. I understand now that you cannot tell when he comes and goes and I understand that the man likes his privacy. I know how he feels. I also like my privacy.

One of those evenings while I was in New York, I was able to get into the audience of the "Tonight Show." The people that wanted to see the show had to stand in line and when all the seats were full, the line was cut. I was lucky. I got in the line early. Anyway, there I was, sitting just a few yards away from my man. I had my briefcase full of Spanish treasure and didn't have enough guts to move. I briefly considered just getting up out of my seat and walking up on stage, but decided I didn't want to spend the remainder of my time in New York City in their jailhouse.

Well, back to the "wait outside by his limo ploy"...Pink Panther, eat your heart out! I waited and I waited and finally, there he was. I walked up to him, introduced myself, and attempted to explain my mission and give him the letter and the pictures. He was quicker with the word than I was. Remember, I was only a young 24 year old kid from the country and he is the world's greatest talk show host. He recommended that I take the envelope to one of the talent scouts the next day and he would look at it after they had a chance to review it. He acted as though he was in a hurry and talked as he was getting into his limo. Before I knew it, he was gone. My pipe dream went up in smoke again.

Well, Johnny, I don't give up. I thought of every possible way to get invited onto your show. My next thought would be to write a good book that would help a lot of people. Then, maybe then, you will invite me to your show. Even if it is for the last 30 seconds of your show. I do not want to be on when you have one of your guest hosts. I want to visit with you.

In the beginning, I cannot say what my real motivation was, but now, I would like, one, to be on your show; two, and meet you; three, sell my book to all those that might gain from it; and four, get rich off my book and go fishing. I know one appearance on your show is not going to sell my book. But, it would be a nice send-off.

John, I am much older and wiser now. I have written a great book. The book will help a lot of people. I have waited for twenty years now, and, if necessary, I will wait for another twenty years. By the time I finally get on the "Tonight Show," I hope you are still there and still as funny as always.

I have had over fifty different jobs and occupations. I have lectured at different places around the world. I have counseled professional basketball teams, doctors, lawyers, and U.S. State Dept. officials in time of world crisis. I have counseled Playboy bunnies, housewives, general laborers, criminals, students, children, and at least one Indian chief! I have counseled people from all over the world and have worked with servicemen that have been everywhere, from Pearl Harbor to the Bay of Pigs. I have worked with Vietnam veterans, and former prisoners of war.

I have been in the selling game, selling everything from $0.29 toys to $20,000,000.00 buildings. I have been successful and I have been busted. I have been to jail three times. Once for not having an up-to-date fishing license; once for having a broken turn signal on my car; and the other time, for attempting to sell my wife's San Antonio Spurs game ticket for less than the price marked on the ticket! I learned one thing on those three occasions: DO

NOT, I say, DO NOT, argue with the policeman or the judge! Through my travels, I have gathered enough information to teach the human how to be successful, healthy and happy. With this book, I have made my contribution to society. Now it is time to hang it up and go fishing.

John, through your show, you have helped many people. I know that you would do anything to help your fellow man, because as anyone can see, you are a good person. I have waited and waited and, if necessary, I will continue to wait. I am looking forward to our visit. I will see you on the "Tonight Show."*

*Here we are in the year 2002 and Johnny has retired!

NOTES

CHAPTER 21
THE CHILD

It might be said that a child is nothing more than a totally exposed Subconscious. Therefore, the child needs to be handled with care and affection. He should be told and taught only things that make up the truth. A lie is nothing more than an untruth told to be true. How unfair this is to a child. Whenever this child grows up and becomes an adult, he then, uses what he thinks to be true. If it is not true, then the person is in for a lot of trouble. So, if you have children, or you work with children, teach them that truth is supreme; truth is power; truth is happiness; truth is the total and only answer.

    I get to work with all kinds of children from the ages of 3 to 18. Unfortunately, too many of our children have been lied to and conditioned to fail in every endeavor. Where did all this lousy training come from? The total society was involved: family, church, schools, Hollywood, TV, the newspaper, everywhere.

    Several weeks ago, a young mother brought me her nine-year-old son, who was a chronic thumb sucker. The mother had allowed her child to suck on a pacifier until he was about three years old. As he grew older, whenever the child would cry, the mother would take her son's hand and stick his thumb in his mouth, in order to shut him up. Several years went by and now, at nine years of age, the child continued to suck his thumb and the mother could not understand why. She had inadvertently trained the boy's Subconscious that when he had a "feel-bad," the next step was to suck his thumb. Also, his illogical Subconscious concluded that to get the "feel-good," he must suck his thumb. So, during "feel-bads" and feel-goods," the child sucked his thumb. After I showed the boy how to take control of his Subconscious, he did just that. He took charge of his Subconscious and he no longer sucks his thumb. There is a familiar pattern here. Throughout the years that little Johnny sucked his thumb, he bore the brunt of all the verbal abuse from his parents, the school, and his friends. Whenever he received this verbal abuse, he had a "feel-bad." He did not know how to block those feelings. So, the cycle continued. "Feel bad? Suck your thumb." This negative input got the young boy a genuine "feel-bad" and his Subconscious said, "What can we do for little Johnny to make him feel good?" Answer: "Suck your thumb." This same pattern applies to almost all so-called unacceptable behaviors. Oftentimes, more than you might realize, this is what happens with body dysfunction. In goes the negative. Out comes the body dysfunction.

I advocate a revolution of truth in education to begin from Day One. I support a retraining of the masses, so that all can understand what the real truth is. This transition should be taking place at all levels of life, not just in the schools and not just at the adult level. The first step would be to educate the people as to how the mind works in conjunction with the body. Remember...Only that which is True!

CHAPTER 22

TEENAGERS ARE PEOPLE, TOO!

Everywhere you look, you will find teenagers. Thank the Lord! If this were not the case, the human race would soon fade into the sunset. Regardless of your age, if you are an adult, you were once a teenager. Like it or not, you have been there.

I have heard people sit around and gripe about teenagers doing exactly the things these people used to do when they were young. I truly hope you are not one of those that doesn't have anything better to do than sit around and criticize. Get off your duff and get involved and you may see that some of the things young people are doing are better and a lot more fun than the things you used to do. I am not talking about the illegal activities. I am talking about the "different" things teenagers do, in this day and time. You might learn something and, on the other hand, you may be able to teach something that the teenagers will want to learn. If you sit back and complain, you lose.

Each and every young person that has passed through my office has been very knowledgeable, very capable, and very much aware of the two-facedness of some of the adults in our society. It seems as though when a person becomes an adult, he looks back at the younger person and fails to give him credit for knowing anything. The human mind is very capable of retaining and using information in a rational manner. Yes, it is the adult's place to pass on knowledge that he has learned, but let's do it with respect to the person we are passing it on to.

What have you been teaching your children? I get teenagers in my office that take dope, smoke marijuana, sniff glue, rob, steal, commit acts of violence; you name it. These kids had to learn their traits from someone.

Your job, as an adult, if you plan to live out your life in a peaceful and serene world, is to respect the young person first, not fear him. Teach him the advantages of what you think is right and teach him the disadvantages of those things you consider wrong. Give him a reason as to why you think the way you do. You already know that shoving your ideas down his throat doesn't work. Sometimes a teenager will listen and not argue, but when he does disagree, he may have a point that you need to consider.

Remember that when dealing with the teenager, he or she was raised in a society that taught him to want to know why. So, in order to get favorable results from that teenager, give him a reasonable answer to why you want something done. In the past, I saw my dad, who was a college chemistry professor, make decisions right off the cuff without considering the end results. I am sure all of us have done this many times. Remember, what we did in the past is unimportant. What is important is how we do it now.

Also, remember the bear and the cookie. Throw the cookie, then the punch. Example: The cookie: "You have been reading this chapter and you are a very smart and capable person and I like you very much." The punch: "Now, do as I have asked you to do." For the teenager not to do what you have asked him to do, he will have to conclude to *self* that he is not smart and not capable. Obviously, he is not going to do that. He will not turn against himself.

If you give the bear the cookie, he will not give up the cookie. The bear will take a few punches without fighting back. If the cookie is too small and the punch is too hard, the bear will fight and you will lose. If the cookie is too large and the punch too light, the bear wins and you lose.

Treat your teenagers with love and respect and it will be returned to you. Try it!

NOTES

CHAPTER 23

THE SIMPLE HANDSHAKE, PLEASE

Because people are generally reactors and not thinkers, one of the most important things that a person should learn to use early in life is the simple, standard, firm-grip handshake. When you have that kind of handshake, an introduction or meeting with another person automatically opens with a strong, positive beginning.

There are many things that can result from a good, traditional handshake. One is that the other party will probably conclude that he is dealing with a person who has had experience in dealing with many people, and that he had, therefore, better be on his toes. We are trained that strength is power and strength is good. If the other party thinks that you are a strong individual, he may be less apt to try to take advantage of you. In this world today, the weak do not survive. So, think of yourself as strong and you will be.

When you use the traditional handshake, make it a good one. Many people will offer a limp, drab hand with lifeless fingers for you to shake. Some people put out their hand as though they are afraid that they're never going to get it back or they are afraid that they're going to get it chopped off. It doesn't matter if you are male or female, young or old. Develop a firm and positive handshake. Practice on your family and your friends. It makes no difference who you practice with. Just do it.

If you are one of those people with sweaty hands, when you use what I have taught you in this book, your hands will stop sweating. If, for some reason, you are unsuccessful at drying up your sweaty palms, keep applying what you have learned in this book and soon you will experience success. But, if you are going to stick out a wet hand, at least, make it firm. No one likes a wet, lifeless handshake.

I like to tell stories about my good friends, so here is another one. I used to call on hospitals in my early years, when I worked for a medical supply company. I knew one purchasing agent that whenever I reached out to shake his hand, all I could ever get was four fingers. It is a funny feeling to just shake a man's fingers! I thought and planned every week how I could get a firm grip out of this man, but, to this day, when I shake his hand, all I get is fingers.

Many good things can happen when you use the traditional, firm handshake. Remember, your Subconscious records everything you do and once your Subconscious records that you can be strong in your handshake, it will support you in other areas where strength and confidence are called for.

CHAPTER 24
PLEASE DO NOT BOTHER ME. I AM NOT DEAD

People continually call my office in hopes of eliminating the fear of going to the dentist or of going to the hospital for necessary or elective surgery. With all the horror stories one hears today about someone going to the dentist for oral surgery and dying while in the chair, and others that go into surgery in the hospital and come out as a corpse, it is no wonder. Fear is nothing more than a message from the Subconscious that says, "Look out, you are going to get hurt."

I have had people in my office prior to every type of surgery that you could imagine. When the Subconscious is properly conditioned, oral surgery, general surgery, or specialized surgery is a snap. When you use what I have taught you in this book, you can go through your surgery with flying colors.

I am reminded of a situation where a gentlemen who worked at an auto parts store was complaining to me about being afraid of going in for his open-heart bypass surgery. At first, when I told him what I could do for him, he was quite skeptical. I told him that if he didn't trust me, he could come to see me, and, after his surgery, if he thought that he had benefited by what I had to offer, then he could pay me.

I took him through the exact program that I take everybody through, and I explained how he was the one that caused his problem. He was angry and upset all the time and he generally had a lousy outlook on life. The body cannot handle that kind of constant negative input. In his case, it caused heart problems. In another person, it may cause ulcers, migraines, backaches, etc. The body can break down in any number of ways.

After I finished with him, he was a totally changed person. He became very relaxed, eliminated all his fears and replaced them with commands to his Subconscious that were to be carried out before, during, and after surgery.

Besides the suggestions that I gave him in the office, he was also to command to himself before surgery, that his body stay perfectly healthy and relaxed, while waiting to go into surgery. Since the surgical procedures were to be carried out by known competent doctors, he might as well stay relaxed. There was to be minimal bleeding and no body trauma, resulting from the surgery. And, after surgery, he was to heal many times faster than the ordinary person. One very important command that must always be given is: "If any of the hospital or surgical staff accidentally says something negative about my condition during surgery, I am to disregard it completely." Many times, doctors have been known to slip and say, while the patient is under the anesthetic, "This poor fellow won't make it." The Subconscious hears this, even though the patient is under the anesthetic, and the command could be carried out. Remember, we were trained to believe everything that our doctor tells us!

Well, as always, this patient did exactly as I suggested. He went through the surgery with flying colors; came out of recovery sooner than was expected and was dismissed from the hospital much sooner than his fellow patients.

Because the hospital personnel might think that he was dead while he was in his perfect state of concentration (hypnosis), I had my secretary type a pink 3" by 5" card for him that he could lay on his chest. The card read: "Please do not disturb. I am not dead. I am doing my relaxation exercises. If it is really important, tell me and I will wake up." Also, the nice part was it always got a good laugh and laughter is good for the soul.

A doctor told me that he knew an anesthesiologist that would whisper in his patient's ear while he was on the operating table, "Pay your anesthesiologist first. Pay your anesthesiologist first." The doctor claimed that he never had any trouble with collections! Obviously, this doctor knew that the Subconscious never sleeps.

As you can see, everybody needs to know how to use the tools they were born with. Everyone has a Subconscious; so do you. Use it to your best advantage.

NOTES

CHAPTER 25

PRESCRIPTION DRUG ABUSE

I am going to tell you some things that may be contested by some members of the medical community, but that is o.k. with me. Maybe when we take a closer look at the situation, we can start gaining some real ground in the prescription drug abuse problem.

You can read the papers and watch the television set, and all you seem to see nowadays is that the drug abuse problem is getting worse. I'm here to tell you that drug abuse is not the problem, even though the general public thinks so. Drug abuse is only the symptom. The problem is that members of the general public, during their growing-up years, were not taught to think. That's right. People were trained to be reactors, not thinkers. If you have not changed yet as a result of reading this book, you are probably still a reactor. Reacting can be dangerous, but thinking can keep you safe.

Because people were primarily trained to react, this is often what they do. Many times, these reactions are negative and along with these negative reactions come the "feel-bads." Because the Subconscious will constantly try to protect you, it will search out anything that will eliminate these terrible "feel-bads."

How many thousands of times have you heard someone say, "If you feel bad, why don't you take something that will make you feel good?" If you tell your doctor that you feel bad, he will get out his pen and prescription pad and write you a prescription for something to take. He was not trained to know how to sit down with you and figure out why you have the "feel-bad." He was trained to give you drugs for the symptom. Do not misunderstand me. The medical community has accomplished brilliant and amazing things, but I think that there are areas of medicine that need a closer look.

I think 90% of all medical problems will be eliminated when we teach the general populace to think and to understand how the mind and body function together.

So, if you have a drug problem, the easiest and cheapest way to eliminate the drugs from your life is to contact your doctor and explain to him that you have changed the way you think about yourself and your environment, and that you are going to give up the drugs. Explain to him that the only drugs you will use will be for convenience only. Tell him you are now in charge of your own health. And while you are changing your way of thinking and living, allow him to monitor your actions. The reason I ask you to do this is that I am not a doctor and I do not have the powerful American Medical Association to back up what I say. If you die in the hands of your doctor, he has malpractice insurance and the AMA to back him up. I am not going to put my life on the line for yours. I am going to take care of me first. If I were to accidentally break a leg, I would go to my doctor and use his services and his medical training, but I would still be in charge of the healing process and my good health.

As you become changed, and you can become changed every moment of your life, you will see that your so-called dependency on drugs will diminish. You will feel better. You will look better. Your life will be smoother and everything will be fine. You can do it. Just follow what I teach you in this book. Change your life.

CHAPTER 26

YOU CAN ELIMINATE PAIN AND DISEASE

There are many people in the world who are experiencing what is called "chronic pain." In many of these cases, the doctors seem to find no logical reason for the pain. In others, the pain seems to be a result of either a new or an old injury. Sometimes it is a result of cancer or other disease. There can be pain as a result of physical body injury, such as a strained muscle, a broken leg or a cut on the hand. There can be pain as a result of an illness, such as a sore throat, a chest cold, and the list goes on. The Subconscious sends out a signal that something has been damaged.

What may have happened in these situations is the body has experienced contamination, such as in cross-infection, or exposure to a chemical that it is not normally accustomed to dealing with. When the body then attempts to adjust to these situations, sometimes this results in pain. The patient can feel the change taking place whenever the body tries to adjust to the foreign substance. However, when the body is perfectly relaxed and there is perfect circulation, the body can fight off the foreign substance easier, with its own immune system.

I am not saying to give up doctors. I am saying to use your doctor and his vast knowledge, as a convenience. That is the way most doctors would like it. We are lucky to have the medical profession and all of its fantastic achievements. Remember, when you walk into your doctor's office, the responsibility for your health is on your shoulders, not his. He is there to aid and assist you.

One of the newest concepts today in dealing with chronic pain is that of the so-called Pain Clinics. These Pain Clinics are cropping up all over the country and they are making new strides daily. Chronic pain is one of the easiest body dysfunctions to eliminate. You must realize that I deal with this sort of thing on a daily basis and I understand it. If you are experiencing chronic pain, read this book carefully. After you understand and use the procedures that I have outlined in this book, you can eliminate your chronic pain.

By understanding the pain and its possible source, it is very easy to eliminate it. Without the mind, it would be impossible to experience the pain. This statement may seem to be a little basic, but it is first necessary to understand why pain exists.

Pain is nothing more than a signal that there is something wrong in the body. Guess what! The thought process also takes place within the confines of the body. Therefore, there could be something wrong with your way of thinking.

When I say there could be something wrong with your thought process, I simply mean that you may be perceiving too many things in your life to be "no-good." You may even be thinking that you are not the person you want to be. This type of perception of self is not wise. The Subconscious only understands *yes* or *no*, and if you see yourself as "no-good" or not as you want to be, you are creating a *yes* and *no* at the same time, and that creates conflict for the Subconscious. The Subconscious sends you a "feel-bad" as a warning signal to stop you from criticizing yourself.

"I am no-good." This is a negative statement with the direct command, "I am." When you command "I am" in the negative form, you will get the negative feeling that goes with the command. Also, because you are a person that was trained not to think, but to react, you will probably react like a negative person. Negative actions, in turn, will get you negative reactions. The cycle continues.

"I am not the person I want to be" is also a negative command. "I want to be" is a statement about the future. The Subconscious Mind cannot deal with things that do not exist and the future does not exist yet. When the future gets here, it will be a NOW.

Planning is o.k. "I want to be" is not a command. "I am planning now to be" is the right way to command the positive. The proper thought process to create the "feel-good" should be a command like the following: "It does not matter what has happened in the past. It does not matter what I have done. I am changed now. I am changed by my own choice. I am a good person now. My past is just that, the past."

You use the same procedure for eliminating pain that you use in eliminating any body dysfunction. You are not to mention the words, "pain" or "discomfort." Speak only in terms of the body being perfectly relaxed and healthy and that you are getting healthier every day.

A very religious man came to see me because of a tremendous and constant pain in his back. The doctors had tried everything that they knew to do. He came to me as a last resort. I usually get people after they have tried everything and nothing has worked for them. I should have gotten them first. No, that is not true. They should have known and used the *Laws of the Subconscious*. Then, they would not have to depend on the doctors or me to guide them toward good health.

Anyway, this man with the chronic pain was a retired

serviceman that had survived two wars, walked away from plane crashes, and seemed to be able to handle any situation that he found himself in. He was probably one of the most Christian men that I have ever met and he was one fine, all-around good citizen. He was an excellent father, grandfather and husband. I could find no faults in this man. He seemed to be the perfect guy.

After working with this man for three or four sessions, I finally found what was causing the problem. Actually, the problem was two-fold. One was the way he talked and thought about himself, and the other was what he thought about the people he associated with.

When someone would ask him, "John, how are you doing today?" he would reply, "Poorly, thank you. Praise the Lord." I said, "John, do you realize that you are reinforcing the fact that you do not feel well, every time someone greets you with a pleasant 'Hello'?" John, trying to be an honest man, would tell them exactly how he felt. I said, "John, turn around that statement and next time someone asks how you are doing, regardless of how you feel, say, 'Fantastic, thank you. I feel fantastic. Praise the Lord.'" Just that one change put a smile on John's face that you could not wipe off.

The way he thought about the people he worked with was causing him fear. He was always afraid that he was not humble enough and that people might think that he was not doing his job properly. This man allowed his impression of the thoughts of others to rule his life. There is absolutely no way you can control the thoughts of other people. He said, "I want them to think well of me," rather than saying to himself, "I will do my job the best I know how. If they choose to think well of me, that is o.k. If they choose not to think well of me, that is o.k., too." It is unfortunate that people are trained the way they are. I am writing this book in the best way that I know how. If you like the book, fine. If you do not like the book, that is fine, too. I like it.

Back to John, As a result of my time with him, he finally stopped being concerned about the uncontrollable thoughts of others. He continued to do his job, as he was trained to do. He enjoyed doing it and his pain subsided.

Here is my message now to all the Pain Clinics around the world. There is a reason for that pain. Find the reason in the patient's head. Rationalize it and the pain will go away. If the person is sick with the flu or pneumonia or a backache or a stomach ache, there is a reason why, and a big part of this reason is stored in his mind. Obviously, the Pain Clinics are doing fantastic work and the people that work in the clinics are doing a great job. Now, let's do a greater job.

If you have pain, you must determine the cause. Keep searching for the cause until you find it. If you cannot find the cause and you still have pain, there are several things that you say to your Subconscious Mind while in the hypnotic state, as well as in the Conscious state. Say to yourself:

"I only live in this moment. The things that have happened to me in the Past mean absolutely nothing, and the reason they mean absolutely nothing is: The Past is the Past and it cannot be changed."

The Past is like a simple broken egg. Once it has happened, it is simply unimportant. The things that were said and done by other people were said and done because they may not have understood their own feelings.

I have found that probably one of the biggest problems that people have is they feel that their parents did not love them. So, the following is to be commanded to the Subconscious concerning your parents, regardless of whether you knew them or not. Each and every parent, regardless of what he did and said, somewhere inside his heart had love for his child. Even though he may not have known how to show that love, it was there. Just as I love a child of mine, regardless of what that child does. I may not like what the child does, but I love the child as a human being. And, even though I may not know how to show that love, it is there.

If you have been unable to show your love to a person and you want to show that love, give yourself the following commands: "The Past is the Past. I now can and do show my love." Surprise! It works.

You cannot change the Past, so command yourself to remember only the good times of the Past. Tell yourself that if the uncomfortable memory of the Past comes to mind, it will not bother you, because now you are a perfectly relaxed, 100% healthy person, and you are not bothered by anything. Even if you are reading this while in a hospital bed, you must still say the words that you are 100% healthy and absolutely nothing bothers you; and the Subconscious will do everything in its power to make you that way.

You were probably trained (from your negative past) to say, "When I am well and out of this hospital, I will feel better." This is asinine. Say to yourself, "I am well now and I feel great and I do not worry about the future, because there is no such thing as worry. There is no stress in my life, because stress does not exist. I have no problems. I only have situations and I either deal with those situations or I do not. Whatever the case, I simply choose not to be bothered." You tell yourself that you plan for the future, if you so desire, but you do not worry about anything. Eliminate the word, "worry" from your vocabulary. If you will follow these simple steps, you will see your pain vanish.

You Can Eliminate Pain and Disease

It must be understood that body dysfunction and disease can be caused from cross-infection from bacteria and viruses. If you use your head, you can protect yourself from cross-infection. Stay away from the unclean and contagious. If you don't know what is unclean and contagious, ask for advice and counseling from your doctor. Ignorance is no excuse. Knowledge is everything.

If you happen to have a disease, it is your responsibility to eliminate it. You will eliminate the disease as easily as wiping dust off a table. However, you must continue your medical treatment, as an aid to the healing process. Your doctor knows what he is doing. There are different ways of imagining the disease out of your body. Different schools of thought all use different types of suggestions. Some say it is the movies of your mind. Some say to imagine the disease being eaten away for certain factions. It makes no difference what mental procedure you go through. Just go through it. Select a procedure that is comfortable for you, but always imagine in the thought process that the disease is leaving your body and it is getting smaller and smaller each day.

There is absolutely no reason to have disease. From this day forward, condition your own mind. Do not allow the world to condition it for you. If you are in the learning process, which we all are, choose to make the learning process positive, refusing all negatives. Put away all antiquated theories as to what causes what, as far as your body is concerned, and control your own body with your mind.

It makes no difference where the illness or dysfunction shows up. You do not need it. So, evaluate your thinking process and ask your Subconscious Mind what is wrong in your life. If your Subconscious Mind says anything regarding conditions, thoughts, people, ideas, or whatever else, turn it around and make a positive of it. See the positive side of it or put it away forever, because the Past and those things that happened in the Past, simply do not exist. If you try to predict the Future by saying, "What if I do so and so next week?" you are wasting your thought process. You cannot predict the Future and I have never met anyone yet that could.

If you are healthy, put your foot down and say, "I am always healthy. I never get sick. I refuse to get sick. There is absolutely nothing that can upset me. I am 100% relaxed. I am 100% calm and I control my own thinking. I simply choose to feel good all of the time. I only use positive thoughts and I only think in positive ways and I always see the positive side of each and every situation."

At this point in writing this book, I thought I had completed the chapter and my wife said the chapter needed more of a conclusion, so she wrote the following:

"You will never have health problems again, if you do what I've told you to do. What do you have to lose?"

I will show you here an accidental mistake. What my wife should have written is, "You will always be healthy, if you do and think as I have told you. You have everything to gain."

COMMENTS FROM A CLIENT

The first appointment was not what I had thought it would be and I was not going back. I followed Tom Ray's direction and by the time of my next appointment, I was ready to go back. I could feel the difference in my outlook. Each time I went after that, I was happy to have gone and was glad Tom Ray was keeping in touch. My concentration increased and I was better able to follow Tom Ray's suggestions.

I now look forward to doing things. Planning for the future has been increased each day. At the time of my first appointment with Tom Ray, I felt so bad and had been unable to plan for the next day. The pain in my face has left and I eat with pleasure.

* * *

NOTES

CHAPTER 27

PARALYSIS IS NOT NECESSARY

For practical purposes, let us categorize paralysis in two different ways. Primarily, the doctors will say that there can be paralysis due to medical reasons and also for psychosomatic reasons. Unless the limb is so completely deformed that it is not mechanically possible to move like a normal limb, I believe that the limb can be made to function normally.

One case that I had the opportunity to work with concerned a lady who was approximately 45 years old. She originally came to me to stop smoking. Her paralysis was in her right arm and leg. She could walk, but she would drag her foot, as she attempted to step with her right leg. Her right hand and arm were almost useless. She had very little strength in her arm and leg, but I knew that with the right approach, she could regain the use of her limbs.

After discussing her paralysis briefly, telling me that she had become paralyzed at the age of 13, she then indicated that there was no apparent cause for the paralysis.

During the age regression process (the process of taking a person back through his Memory Bank while in the deep, relaxing state on the couch), she told me when and under what conditions she first had trouble. The first time she could remember having a problem with strength in her limbs occurred during a gym class in high school. The gym teacher was showing the class how to make a human pyramid and she had been selected to be the student on the very top. She was not at all athletic and she was afraid of what might happen if she fell. During the age regression process, she remembered there was a particular day where she worried constantly of what might happen in gym class, if they had to make the human pyramid again. She kept saying, while she was on the couch, "I cannot do it. I cannot do it. I am scared." There was a moment, that day, when she experienced her first symptoms of paralysis.

As I continued to ask her questions, she told me that soon after this first experience with paralysis, she was walking home with some friends after a school dance and the problem came up again. That night, she had not danced with anyone and her friends laughed and joked at her, as young people often do. For some strange reason, her Subconscious took a beating, because of the harassment and caused her to start dragging her foot. She had the feeling as though her foot was "going to sleep." Everybody has experienced a leg or arm going to sleep when the circulation is cut off, so it seemed not to be unusual at the time for her, but it got worse. Her friends meant no harm, but her Subconscious took a beating. She did not know how to handle the kidding. If you do not dismiss the kidding, the Subconscious takes it for fact.

By the time she got home, she literally had to crawl up the steps. She had been totally unable to walk and she had to knock on the door to let her mother know she was home. She remembers skinning her hands and knees, as she crawled up the steps. When her mother answered the door, she was obviously wondering why her child was on her hands and knees. Her mother told her to get up and that there was absolutely nothing wrong with her. Her mother questioned her as to what had happened, and obviously, nothing happened that the girl could relate. So the mother, being a wise old bird, said, "Quit crying. There is absolutely nothing

Paralysis Is Not Necessary

wrong with you," and, surprisingly enough, the young lady was able to start moving her hand, foot and leg again.

I would imagine that the wheels started turning, in the girl's mind and consciously, the girl became worried. I am sure that at this time fear set in, because within a few days, she was paralyzed again. The paralysis did not leave, until she came to me, approximately 25 years later. Her right arm and right leg were a rather bluish color, as a result of obviously poor circulation. If you restrict the circulation in one of your limbs, not only does it get cold, but also it gets a "gone to sleep" feeling, like a numbing sensation. Not only were both her right hand and right leg blue, but also it seemed that she was not getting adequate circulation. I am not a doctor, so it would be difficult for me to explain the way in which the blood vessels that feed the arm and leg were constricted. In fact, this is a backwards way to approach the problem.

So, at this point in time, I decided if the hand and the leg were not getting the proper circulation, we would command the Subconscious to correct the problem. As a result of the poor circulation, the paralysis in the hand and leg made them a cooler temperature than the normal hand and leg. I decided to raise the temperature of the paralyzed hand and leg by simply having the young lady visualize a warm blanket around the leg and the arm. The lady then, during hypnosis, felt the heat of the imaginary blanket. She felt the heat run through her leg and arm. That was the only suggestion on that day that I made concerning the cold, paralyzed limbs, because she had come to see me for the purpose of stopping smoking, not dealing with the paralysis. The next day, she came back, and I could not believe my eyes! Not only did she have a little more mobility in her limbs, but the color of the skin on the paralyzed limbs was identical to the color in her other limbs!

This is what I think happened. The body is full of tiny blood vessels and veins running through the tissue and the muscles, feeding the system. If there is tension, the muscles tighten and restrict the blood flow. It makes no difference what really happened internally, however. What is important is that there was a change. And, the change was for the better. So, if you are paralyzed or partially paralyzed, try every conceivable thought process to increase the health of that limb. You can use movies of the mind, imagination, word pictures, thought processes of any kind, but you use the words as though the fact had already taken place.

What happens is the Subconscious says, "O.K., I will produce for you what you tell me." In some cases, you will find immediate changes. If you say in your mind, "It is not working, it is not working," just remember that the Subconscious Mind will give you what you ask for. It will give you: "It is not working." So, you must continue to give the positive commands to your body that you are healthy; that you are relaxed; that the movement is returning to your limbs. You must say, "is returning," not "will return." If you have been paralyzed for some time, you will find that after your initial movements, your muscles will get sore, but you will tell yourself that it is not sore; it is the healing process, and you are to discount the soreness. You must, consciously, in the waking state, reinforce these positives, because YOU are responsible for your own health---not your doctor, not your friends, not your parents, and not your children.

You are responsible. You use your doctor for a supplement. You control your mind and body and no one else does. No one controls your body and mind but you, and you can even use the old phrase of the late Emil Coue, "I am getting better every day in every way." If you have a spinal injury and the doctor said to you, "You will never walk again," say to the doctor, "Doctor, I will walk again." If the doctor said to you that because of a stroke, part of your brain is dead, discount what he says, because there have been too many cases that have turned around and the person was normal again. The brain does not die as long as you're breathing. So, whenever you accidentally get a negative from your doctor, even though he is trying to help you, say to your doctor: "No, thank you, Doctor, I am becoming a normal and healthy person again, because I control my body and my mind." Then, do it, because the Subconscious Mind does as it is told.

  Case in point: A 36-year old man came to see me, and he was paralyzed from his shoulder to his fingertips on his left side. He explained to me that he had a stroke and that the doctor told him that he would be paralyzed in his left arm and hand the rest of his life. That one statement alone, reinforces the fact that many people in this world will remain paralyzed. The doctors were taught in medical school that a stroke kills part of the brain that operates that part of the body. I believe that is incorrect.

  I have seen too many cases where the limbs returned to normal after several hypnotic sessions, when the Subconscious was told that the arm was o.k., and that the body was healthy, etc. In the particular case of the 36-year old man in the stroke situation, I determined that the stroke was caused as a result of the way the man thought. He was constantly worried about his wife running around on him. When he explained to me the way he felt, it is a wonder the man is not dead. Anyone that would allow himself to become sick as a result of the actions of others, obviously, is thinking backwards.

His doctor had told the man that there was no hope; not to even consider physical therapy; to just give up and face the fact that he could never use the arm and hand again. We are trained to believe that the doctor knows everything there is to know about the body. And we are trained to accept everything the doctor says. If the doctor says there is no hope, then there is no hope, according to the Subconscious Mind. It is time to go one step further and demand that our doctors understand the *Laws of the Subconscious*. Rather than entrust our lives to doctors, which is absolutely incorrect, we should entrust our lives to ourselves, under the doctor's supervision.

Our medical communities have done fantastic things and we should be thankful for what they have done. But hypnosis should be used hand in hand with medicine, rather than the way it is used now. Paralysis is not necessary. Sickness is not necessary. Ill health of any kind is not necessary. Make yourself well and keep your body healthy by seeing pictures in your mind of your body being completely healed. Put your life in your own hands now, where it belongs, and do something positive about your health.

CHAPTER 28

TOM RAY'S COMA THEORY

One day I read an article in a local newspaper about a person who was in a deep coma and had been there for approximately 40 days. The doctors (according to the article) needed a miracle. I do not believe in miracles. I just believe in getting results. I reached for the phone and called one of the doctors that the article had named. I explained to the doctor about a theory of mine. I was very eager to try the theory. He needed a miracle and I needed a subject. (I will explain the theory, later on in this chapter.) He indicated that there was the possibility that my theory might work. At this point, he was willing to try anything to save the patient.

After I explained what I thought, he said he might have me work with the patient and he would call me back the following evening to let me know. He did not call the following evening and I thought he must not have believed me, so I called again. He indicated that he would bring me in on the case and he said he would call me back in the next couple of days. He never returned my call. I believed strongly that my theory would work, so I called him a third time. This time, he apparently realized that I was serious about what I thought might work and he invited me to be in on the case.

The patient was in another city, so I made my plane reservations and left as soon as I could. When I arrived, he and another doctor met me at the airport around midnight. We went straight to the hospital, where everyone in the family was waiting. Apparently, the doctor had explained why I was coming to town and the patient's whole family was there to greet me. I knew before I started working with the person in the coma that I must find out as much as I could about him, in the short time that I had. I was fortunate enough to get to talk with all the family, his children, his brother and a sister-in-law. I was able to talk with everyone, except the patient's father. The patient was about 49 years old. I spent about an hour and a half talking to each member of the family. By that time, it was about 2:30 a.m., and I had talked to everyone and had gotten as much information as I could. Now, it was time to go talk to the coma patient. This episode appeared to be so far out in left field that it didn't even seem reasonable to try, but, thank God, I have never been afraid to experiment with the unknown nor have I ever been afraid to try something new.

I walked into the Intensive Care Unit and saw the patient, with tubes running in and tubes running out. All but one of the doctors that had been on the case had given up. I am not a doctor, but I believe that as long as the heart is beating, there is life in that body.

Now, this is my theory. The Subconscious Mind never sleeps. Since it never sleeps, it can be commanded, even in a coma. Therefore, I could command this man to heal his body and come out of his coma. It is fact that many times, people have had surgery and later recounted things the doctors talked about while doing the operation. This is not always the case, but it has happened. That is why it is so important that during and after each surgery, the right words should be said around the patient, such as: "This patient will recover immediately. This person is very healthy, and when he wakes, and as he heals, he will become stronger after surgery than he was before."

So, based on many existing facts, plus the experience of some of my clients, it is my theory that even while a person is in a coma, his Subconscious can be commanded. Of course, I explained to the doctor that there was a one in a million chance it would work, because I did not want to generate any false hope for the family. After all, this patient had not moved at all, voluntarily, for forty days. Even though it is a fact that you can command the body to heal at a faster rate, and that I believe that the Subconscious Mind never sleeps, it was only my theory that I could command this patient to heal his body and wake up. I certainly did not expect him to open his eyes immediately. The least I expected him to do was to move in some way or respond to my commands. So, I started talking to him.

    I leaned over the bed so that I could talk directly into his ear and I made very sure that I did not touch the bed. In case he did move, I would be able to see any slight change. His doctor and another physician were there with me and they stood watching, on the other side of the bed. Five minutes into the one-way conversation, and to the amazement of everyone, he moved!

    This is something he had not done in 40 days! Not only did I see him move, but the other people standing there also, saw him move. In addition, his heart rate increased immediately. His heart rate increased just as yours does any time you exert your body in any way. Naturally, this increased heart rate was shown on the monitor. Not only did we see it, it was electronically recorded! I immediately told the doctors not to become too optimistic, because this could have been coincidental. I did not want to generate false hope, but something did happen in that Intensive Care Unit that night.

    I needed to get back to my office in San Antonio, so I decided to make tapes of my voice and leave them to be played at different times during the day.

During the next eight months, the patient progressed to the point that the doctors concluded that his body was perfectly healthy. That means proper brain waves; eyes reacting to light; all body functions working normally. However, this gentleman finally died and I think that he died because he did not want to face certain people in his family. The information I gathered that first night gave me the indication that there was a tremendous battle going on between the man and his father. He just could not face his father. That is my conclusion; an educated guess.

In the beginning, I wanted to bring in a tape of the father's voice saying that the fight was over and everything was clear between the two. The doctors overruled me on this. The next case I take, I will call all the shots or I will not be on the case.

CHAPTER 29

THE CRIMINAL MIND

When I hear someone say that a person has a criminal mind, right away I know that the person making the statement knows little about the mind and how it works.

When a person does something illegal, he is simply doing what he thinks is right at the time. He was conditioned by certain factors he has encountered, to believe that his criminal act is justified. His decision to break the law has nothing to do with the law or even with morals. This decision has to do with what the person perceives to be good for himself, at the time. Therefore, the way to convert a criminal is to recondition his Subconscious to perform satisfactorily in a law-abiding society.

People have sat around and debated on how to correct the crime situation in the world and I am here to tell you that it is very simple. The process has to start with the young child. Condition him to think that staying within the framework of the law in an organized society is the easiest, safest, healthiest, and most productive way to go. Unfortunately, the criminal has been conditioned to believe that crime is fun, easy, more productive, or necessary to survive.

When a person goes to jail, and he is due to get out before he dies, constant reconditioning should be mandatory, in order to return a productive human to society. If you're going to lock a man up, with plans to later return him to society, it would be wise to educate him; show him the easy way to live; show him a healthy way of thinking. While you have him in jail, make him think; make him learn. He should be made to improve his mind. Improving one's ability to think rationally never hurt anyone.

Obviously, there are a lot of fine people out there supervising the detention systems that think they are doing a good job. Look at the statistics and you can see that what they are doing is simply not good enough. Good is not good enough. What we need are results... fantastic results.

Every person is a good person and should be taught or conditioned to live a productively, happy, healthy, life within the framework of an organized society.

Just because a President, or a judge, or a popular public figure breaks the law, that is not a good reason why anyone else should also break the law.

I had a very disturbed 10 year-old boy in my office not long ago, who was very concerned about the problems of the world; the problems that he sees daily in the newspaper and on television. I was amazed that his young mind was so perceptive.

We have taught many of our people to be criminals. They did not arrive on this earth as criminals. Now it is time to teach our children that there is a better way to live. Crime is not necessary.

You are responsible for teaching those around you that honesty is the best policy. Do not rely on your neighbor or your school or your church to teach your children the honest, healthy, fun, productive way to live. YOU DO IT!

CHAPTER 30

PHYSICAL CHILD ABUSE

There is more than one victim in each child abuse case. I have found in my work with the abuser, that he usually is having a battle within himself. Remember when I explained that the Subconscious Mind cannot handle *yes/no* situations? The Subconscious sends out a "feel-bad" directly related to the importance the person puts on the situation. Therefore, if it is a very important *yes/no* situation, you will experience a very big, "feel-bad."

The abuser observes the child in a given situation. If that situation is in direct conflict with what the abuser was taught to think, the *yes/no* situation is recorded. Rather than seeing the situation as a learning situation for the child, as a logical and rational adult should; and rather than stopping and thinking, and correcting the child in a firm, relaxed, loving manner; the person reacts violently to the situation. In many of these instances, the child abuser will only be abusive with one of several children. Regardless of the situation, the child abuser is only reacting; he is not thinking. Animals react. People can learn to think, and that is what this book is all about.

The abuser has allowed his Subconscious to take control of his body, and a child suffers. One young lady who was in my office claimed that her mother would line her children up along the wall and slap each one. If a child flinched, she would hit the child again. To most people, this sounds like child abuse, but this mother, in her own stupid way, was teaching her children to take a punch and survive out there in the cold, cruel world. Unfortunately, this was her way of loving and teaching her children to survive. Child abuse comes in all forms.

Often, the child abuser just thinks that he is taking charge over the child and is teaching the child right from wrong. The abuser, in this case, does not see himself as a cruel person or as an abuser. However, some child abusers are remorseful and later sorry for their actions. They think they just cannot control themselves. Remember, an abuser is not responding to the child. He is responding to old information from the past, which is stored in his Memory Bank.

Any number of things can be taking place in the mind of the abuser when he is beating up on a child. Remember, the Subconscious can be triggered through any of the senses. The abuser hears something, sees something, touches something, smells something, thinks something, that relates back to an old "feel-bad" situation. Then he goes in to his abusive actions to eliminate his own "feel-bad." He is reacting. He is not thinking.

If you are in a situation where you know a person is abusing a child and you allow it to happen more than once, you are just training him to continue. You, in essence, are approving of the abuse, by not taking a stand to prevent it. Whether it is your child or someone else's child, you are responsible to check out the facts. If you are married to a child abuser, take a stand. Would you want someone to stand up for you if you were getting beaten up? If you are afraid of the abuser, you had better get additional help quickly. If not, you lose. And the child surely loses.

Many times, child abuser's spouses will allow abuse of their children because they are down on themselves and fear that they will not get another mate if they lose the one they

Physical Child Abuse

have. They sometimes think that what they have is better than nothing is and they are willing to sacrifice the child because of their own ignorance and greed. If a mother or father allows children in the home to be abused by the other spouse, he or she should also experience the law to its fullest extent. Guilty by submission; guilty by association; guilty for not stepping in and seeking help; guilty, guilty, guilty!

The answer: EDUCATION. Several things should be taught to the child abuser. One: that the child can be damaged physically, mentally, or both. Two: that the abuser does have control over his Subconscious Mind and his actions, even though he thinks he does not. Three: he will surely pay to the full extent of the law for his abusive actions. If, after the abuser is informed of how the mind works and how the law works, he or she continues to abuse the child, the law must prevail. There must be laws and enforcement of these laws in order to maintain an organized, safe society.

I have worked with many abused children, as well as adults who claim to have been abused as children. Some really were abused and others were not. They just thought they were. Fortunately, many were just cases where the person felt that the other children in the family were getting preferential treatment. In about 90% of the cases where the client has brothers and sisters, the client claimed that he always got the short end of the stick. "My older or younger brother or sister always got treated better than I did. They were always getting me into trouble. Mother and Daddy loved them more than they did me." But, every time, and that's every time, I have talked with the other children in the family, the story was just the reverse. They thought they got the short end of the deal. So, if you are sitting there reading this and you think that your parents shortchanged you, you are probably wrong.

I have never, absolutely never, met a mother or father that did not love his or her child. The parents may have been ignorant about teaching and raising children, but they always loved their child. Often, the parents will give more attention to the child they perceive as the weaker one. If they feel that the child needs more help, they will go out of their way to help that child. So, if it appears that you were overlooked, you were not. Your parents probably felt that you were stronger and more capable.

I once had a client who claimed that he was never given the opportunity to be a normal child. His parents were very wealthy and they lived on a vast estate. He had a big lake to fish in and the countryside to play in. But he was never allowed to get dirty. He always had to look neat. Therefore, he didn't feel that he was like other children. This person, as an adult, spent all his time complaining about his childhood. He complained so much that he was unable to function as a normal adult.

It is foolish to sit back and think about things that you cannot change. I have never met a person that could change his childhood.

So goes the case of the person who was truly abused as a child. He or she has not been trained to know that the past is the past and it is foolish to pass judgment on a parent that was ignorant of the ways of good parenting. That child abuser was not an abuser automatically. The world taught him to be the way he is. He is a conditioned animal.

Remember, every child abuser was born on a given day as a tiny baby, knowing nothing. The world took this child and taught him how to react and to not think. The child abuser thinks he is correct. So, if you were abused as a child, decide NOW that you are no longer affected by your past; you are a logical, rational, thinking person that chooses his own feelings; and you will choose only good feelings from now on.

If you sit around and play "poor me," you lose. Determine that you are a product of the way you choose to think today, not the product of your past.

If you are still in a situation that you think is abusive, seek the help of professionals. Consult your teachers, your minister, your friends, your neighbors, and your law enforcement agencies. If you do not get help from one source, go to another. Sooner or later, you will get the help you seek. Refuse to be a victim any longer.

NOTES

CHAPTER 31

MARRIAGE: A TWO-YEAR CONTRACT

I work with many people who are having marriage problems. I guess I have worked with every kind of marriage problem that has ever existed and I can see that a simple solution is needed. I believe there is a simple answer to the "bad-marriage" situation. That answer is to make the marriage a simple two-year legal contract that automatically dissolves at the end of every twenty-four months. This is much more practical than the open-ended contract that is predominately used today. If the marriage contract were to end at a prescribed time, many people would simply let the marriage run out and would not re-up their contract.

The following are my proposals for the two-year contract:

1. The contract would become null and void at the end of twenty-four months and could only be renewed at the courthouse or other designated place. The renewal would require the consent and appearance of both partners. If one or both did not wish to continue the marriage, they could simply not show up for the renewal.
2. If the two parties did not renew the marriage contract within fifteen days from the end of the twenty-four months, the court would divide any property down the middle; one-half for each party, unless separate property rights had been previously designated.
3. Any children would become wards of the state until settlement was made regarding custody.

In the course of my practice, I saw one couple that had been married for 55 years and the wife stated that she had hated every moment of that 55 years. Back in 1935, her boyfriend went to the courthouse and got a marriage license, hoping that his girlfriend would marry him. She, being very naive, thought to herself, "He has the license. I have to marry him." Since she was from the school of thought that marriage is forever, she would not consider divorce. She believed that divorce was immoral and out of the question. If divorce were immoral, a lot of us would burn in Hell. Thank goodness, God forgives. How different this woman's life could have been, if she had contracted for a two-year marriage, rather than a lifetime of marriage to a man she didn't love.

I see many a young lady that marries in order to get out of a bad situation at home. If there were a two-year marriage contract, she might think twice about using marriage in this way and possibly being left single again in two years' time, with no education or means of making a living.

Jealousy seems to be a big problem that a lot of couples experience. Under the two-year marriage contract, if a husband is too jealous, the wife could end the marriage simply by not renewing. Since the jealous husband would be aware of this, he might decide to clean up his act, rather than taking a chance on losing his wife. I once had a young lady in my office who told me that as she was growing up, she learned that jealousy meant you were showing your spouse that you cared. The more jealous she was, the more she was showing him that she loved him. It's kind of stupid, don't you think? People learn some weird ways in this world of ours.

One of the problems that seems to be very common occurs when a couple is married for about 30 years; the children are grown and out of the house; and the husband becomes a "do-nothing." He has his drinking buddies down at the pub. He has his fishing buddies and his boat. He has his easy chair that sets directly in front of the TV. When it comes to being with his wife, talking with his wife, making love to his wife, nothing doing.

I recently had a client who lived under those conditions. Her husband had his boat, his motorcycle, his drinking buddies, and his cabin at the lake, and he would not purchase his wife her own car, even though he was financially able to do so. This had been going on for 30 years. Of course, it is partly her fault for not taking a stand. I think the two-year contract would get her that car.

It is easy to understand why a 100,000 or more women each year simply choose to disappear. They want out of the marriage without going through a hassle. I am sure many men want the same thing. Remember, love is a choice, not an obligation. I do not like the word, "force," but I think this two-year marriage contract would force a lot of people to get along.

An elderly man came to my office with a letter from his doctor, stating that he had several strange problems. The doctor used a lot of those $25.00 medical words in describing his patient's behavior. In doing so, the doctor only stated the symptoms, not the problem. Apparently, the man would not talk to his wife. He would not work. He slept all the time. He would not become involved in anything at all, and he may as well have been a vegetable. In our discussions, the problem finally came out. He could not stand his wife. She was an overbearing nag and constantly criticized him for his actions. He determined in his own infinite wisdom, "If I do nothing, I will not be criticized for making mistakes. If I sleep, I do not have to face her. I can't divorce her. My church would excommunicate me. So, therefore, I will retreat into my shell."

I think this is one of the beginning causes of Alzheimer's Disease. I believe that rather than being a disease, Alzheimer's Disease is the result of a thought process. Everybody experiences not recalling things at one time or another. For instance, the other day, I took a plate out of the kitchen cabinet to put a piece of watermelon on. I cut the melon, put the empty plate into the refrigerator, and was left standing there with the watermelon in my hand. Do I have Alzheimer's Disease? No, I was simply thinking about other things while I was preparing to eat the melon. But, if my wife were to ask my doctor why I did that, he would probably tell her that I was just getting old and forgetful! And, if I heard often enough that I was getting old, senile, forgetful, etc., and if I didn't know how to throw that off, I could easily become that way.

I am sure if you thought about it, you could come up with a thousand good reasons for the two-year marriage. I believe it would encourage better communication between husband and wife. The marriage that continued would likely be stronger, as a result of this increased communication. Maybe we should eliminate the word, "love" and introduce logic and good sense when it comes to marriage. Marriage should be a fun and compatible partnership. When the fun and compatibility is gone and everything has been attempted, in an effort to bring the marriage back together, with no success, then there should be a quick, easy, logical and economical way out...the two-year marriage contract.

CHAPTER 32

STUTTERING IS NOT A SPEECH PROBLEM

Stuttering is not a speech problem. It is the result of an unhealthy thought process. In other words, if the person were completely relaxed and calm, to the point where he chose not to be bothered, he simply would not stutter.

If you are a parent and you have a child that is starting to stutter, you had better find out what the problem is, as quickly as you can. By the way, stuttering is only the symptom, or result. The problem is in the way the child is looking at things, or perceiving things. Instead of telling the child, "Stop stuttering," you should say, "Go sit down. Close your eyes. Relax yourself, and you will speak very clearly." After a while, the child, in his effort to eliminate his stuttering, will learn to relax and will, thereby, eliminate the stuttering altogether. Also, look around the child's environment and look for unrest, loud people, unsafe conditions, child abuse, or ignorant teachers. (Most teachers are doing a good job, but this is a possibility.) Also, take a good look at yourself and see if you are an example of a relaxed, fun-loving parent that your child can look up to.

If you are a teenager or an adult and you stutter, you simply do not have to. It is not hereditary. It is a learned process. Yes, there are such things as deformities inside the mouth that can cause speech problems, but these are rare and can usually be corrected medically. If you stutter at certain times and do not stutter other times, then, obviously, you have allowed your Subconscious to rule your life during the times you do stutter.

Let's imagine that your Subconscious consists of a committee of ten big people that live in your basement. Remember, they are there for your protection. They accept anything you tell them, as truth. They will act on *yes* or *no* commands only. They are not logical. They will run your life using old, untrue information that is stored in your Memory Bank, unless you make conscious decisions. If you allow yourself not to be relaxed and confident in a given situation, your Subconscious committee rushes to the files in your Memory Bank and starts looking for something that will get rid of the nervousness and "feel-bads." While the Subconscious committee is flipping through your memory files, it doesn't have time to help you properly pronounce the words or sometimes even to find the words you would like to speak. By choosing to be 100% relaxed and confident in all situations, your Subconscious is free to be there ready to help you in any endeavor you may pursue.

Also, you need to go back into your Memory Bank and search out the times when you first started stuttering and look for the things you did not like. It may have had nothing to do with your speech. Once you have located these situations that were recorded in your Memory Bank, then see yourself examining those things again, and this time, not being bothered, speaking very clearly in a calm and relaxed manner. Then give yourself a reason as to why it happened and tell yourself that it is no longer important, because you are a changed, relaxed person and that absolutely nothing bothers you. You protect yourself. You keep yourself safe, but nothing bothers you and you always speak clearly. You must tell yourself these things.

Everybody on the face of the earth, that ever uttered a word, probably stumbles or gropes for a word several times, every day of their lives. As you are no longer a stutterer, if you happen to stumble on a word or grope for a word, it is unimportant. Just prevent it from getting out of hand.

NOTES

CHAPTER 33

DREAMS, DREAMS, DREAMS

Waking up from a bad dream and not truly understanding dreams and how bad dreams come about, can be quite an experience. The world is full of fortunetellers and soothsayers that will take your money and still not give you correct information about your dreams. Some of these people will tell you that your dreams are a result of your past misdeeds and that the devil is in your head, striking back at you. Others will tell you that your dreams are predictions of the future. When I say, "fortune tellers and soothsayers," this also includes those guys that have the fancy offices and plush couches, the fancy degrees, and the pinstriped suits. With all their fanfare and their high prices, they are going to try to tell you how to better your life by analyzing your dreams. Those guys are getting rich off your ignorance and they usually don't know what they are talking about, when it comes to dreams.

I would hate to go out and count the books that have been published on the subject of dreams and their causes. Every Tom, Dick, and Harry in the counseling business will give you somewhat of a different story about dreams, but I am going to give you the answer that is the simplest and easiest to believe and understand. I am going to tell you why dreams occur and what they are good for. You do not have to accept what I say, but I know you are a very smart person, so you will consider what I have to say. It is all very logical and simple.

Nighttime dreams come from the Subconscious. Daydreams also come from the Subconscious. When the

Conscious Mind is not active, thoughts flow from the Subconscious in irregular patterns. Remember, the Subconscious is not logical. The Subconscious also houses your Memory Bank, which contains a vast amount of information. When you dream at night, the Subconscious is sending out information in semi-organized patterns; information that has been previously thought in a conscious manner. As an example, recently I talked to an old school buddy that I had not seen in some time. A couple of days later, I dreamed about him. Of course, this is not always the case. You may dream about someone or something that you have not thought of in quite some time.

When a person has a bad dream, it may come from either a recent or an old experience that was not pleasant. It could result from conflict experienced anywhere---school, home, or any number of places. Or it may not even have anything to do with the real world. If the person consciously continues to think only unhappy thoughts, then the chances of having bad dreams increase. The conscious thoughts bring that old information out of the Memory Bank vaults and put it up on the shelf where it surfaces very easily during sleep.

Some of our war veterans that still have bad dreams have not consciously put the war behind them. I talked with one the other day that is still having nightmares relating to World War II. He keeps conjuring up thoughts about things that he was exposed to over 40 years ago. It seems like a waste of the thought process to me. If he says that he can't put those thoughts away, he is wrong. Remember, what you think is your choice.

If you have bad dreams or a constantly recurring bad dream, you are consciously keeping it on the front shelf of your Memory Bank by making that dream important. More often than not, fear of the bad dream creates even more bad dreams. Dreams are of no importance and should be handled in that fashion. If you conclude to yourself that dreams are meaningless and that they have no value, and that dreaming is for fun only, your dreams will soon change to pleasant experiences.

The Subconscious can be triggered by thought, and any slight thought could trigger any type of dream. If a person of any age has constant, daily negative thoughts, this could trigger bad dreams. Or the person could have negative thought patterns and actually not have bad dreams. In other words, dreams are not much good for anything. They are not predictable. If the person is having excessive bad dreams, he had better clean up his conscious thinking habits. He can do this by using what I teach in this book.

I dream every night and I enjoy my dreams. I enjoy them because I see them as free movies or adventures provided for me by my Subconscious. I have had my share of bad dreams, but why should I get upset over irregular patterns of information provided to me by my illogical Subconscious Mind? The whole idea is to conclude to be happy regardless, and to conclude to Self that you have only happy dreams. Remember, stay within the Laws of the Subconscious. The Subconscious does as it is told. So, conclude that you have only good dreams.

NOTES

CHAPTER 34

HIT IN THE FACE BY A YELLOW SCHOOL BUS

Some people do get hurt accidentally from time to time and it is necessary to know how to take care of your body and to know how to speed the healing process.

My wife and I have six children (his and hers) and we often go on picnics or camping trips together. You can imagine what it is like when our six children and some of their friends go along. It is not wise to try to transport that many people in a mini-van, so I set out to find a school bus that would suit our needs.

I was visiting a friend's brother one day and there, off in the trees, almost hidden by the underbrush, was an old yellow school bus. The wheels in my head started turning and I asked if I could see the bus. The man that was storing the bus told me that it had been converted into a camper by a group of guys that once had a country and western band. As you can see, the plot thickens.

After wading through the brush and the briars, I finally made it to the spot where it appeared that the old bus had rested since the beginning of the Industrial Revolution. Not only was it a mess, it looked as though chickens, goats, and every other varmint in South Texas, at one time or another, had made their homes in that bus. I am a fairly good shade tree mechanic and I could see that it would be a lot of fun fixing it up. My wife told me that I was crazy and needed to be locked up in a home somewhere! I asked the man if he would sell me the bus. He said that he would take $1500.00 for his beautiful bus camper. When my wife heard what the man said and saw the gleam in my eyes, she knew for sure that she was in for some strange times.

That day, I happened to be driving an old black Cadillac that I had purchased from a local funeral home. I told the man that I had a beautiful Cadillac classic and that I would trade him for the old, junky bus. In any horse trade, you make out that your horse is a Kentucky Derby Winner, even though it may be swayback with no teeth and a lame leg. I knew that I would not be cheating my friend's brother, because he was a part-time mechanic, himself.

He indicated that he would be in favor of the deal, but the bus actually belonged to his mother and I would have to show her my Cadillac before we could trade. I knew of his mother and I knew that the lady was blind. Bless her heart! Here she was, going to make a decision on a horse trade and she could not even see the horse. The son suggested that I give her a ride around the block in the Cadillac and let her decide for herself. Well, good or bad, most Cadillacs ride the same, and I knew I owned the old bus.

My old Cadillac did not look too bad, and when we made the trade, I am sure that the man and his mother felt that they had gotten the better end of the deal. Well, I am here to tell you that I am probably one of the world's best horse traders. I got what I went after, and he got my old Cadillac.

I put gas and a battery in the old bus and proceeded to drive it to the house. After all was said and done, I drove it part of the way and I dragged it the rest of the way, but I had my bus. It would provide ample transportation for my family and any extra kids that might want to go along.

We made several trips in the old yellow bus before we decided to paint it like the Partridge Family's bus: patchwork

Hit In The Face By A Yellow School Bus

quilt colors. I purchased about 15 different cans of spray paint and began to give the old rusty yellow bus a new look. After I finished painting, it was not a new look; it was a strange look.

Whenever we would go somewhere in the old bus, I would usually wear faded jeans, an old T-shirt, and a red headband with a turkey feather stuck in the back. I loved it. The kids enjoyed it. And everywhere we went, people would stare. We had a blast!

Now for the part where I got hit in the face by a yellow school bus. I was working under the bus, replacing the worn-out clutch pedal return spring. I was using a tire iron to replace the spring, when the spring slipped. The tire iron also slipped, and then, it hit me right in the face. Ouch!

I grabbed my face and thought to myself, "Go into hypnosis, go into hypnosis. I am o.k., I am o.k. There is no pain. There is no damage. I am o.k." I went through this procedure for about 30-45 seconds, while lying there under the bus, with my hands covering my face. I crawled out from under the bus and I seemed to be fine. My face felt a little numb, but I felt fine. My nose began to run a little and when I put my hand up to my nose, there were a few drops of blood. When I looked at my face in the side mirror on the bus, I saw a gash on my lip, about an inch long and an eighth of an inch wide. The gash went from my upper lip to the base of my nose.

I started talking to myself again: "Cut, close. No bleeding. I am o.k. There is no infection. There is no swelling. Heal." The Subconscious understands the word, "heal." After this 20 or 30 second session, I went on about my work. I did not take the time to wash or clean the cut, because it appeared to be a clean separation and there was no dirt in the cut. I continued my work and soon forgot about what I had done to my face. (By the way, do not do as I did. Always clean a cut and use a disinfectant or a germicide.)

This all happened about one or two o'clock in the afternoon and, by sundown, when I went in for dinner, the cut was completely closed, and the only thing that was visible was a small, dark blood line where the cut had been.

The following day, I was having dinner at the local fish place and I met an old school buddy that had been in a chemistry class with me. He is now a physician. I proceeded to tell him about the incident. He looked at the cut and said it appeared as though it had been healing for about a week! In reality, it had been only about a day and a half since the incident happened.

By the next day, the cut was completely healed and the only sign left was a slightly pink area where the cut had been!

Ladies and Gentlemen! The body has a tremendous ability to repair itself. Command it and it is so. I like to think that I am a practical man, and even though I was born in Texas, I am from Missouri when it comes to practical things. I have to see it to believe it. Had I not seen what happened, and actually experienced the situation myself, I would not have believed it. The only thing that happened in this situation was that my Subconscious Mind took the orders that I gave it. As a result, as you will remember from the earlier chapters, the Subconscious Mind gave me exactly what I asked for. Had I said, "It is not working. It is not working," the Subconscious Mind would have said, "You are right. It is not working."

The second major time that I used hypnosis to repair my body was when I was working on one of my used cars. Fortunately, I have enough money to buy a new car, but I refuse to buy a new car. If I bought a new car, I wouldn't have anything to work on. My wife does not care at all for that philosophy. Anyway, I was under the hood of my 1972 Cadillac, which was another old funeral car; a big black one, very appropriate for a hypnotist. I was working on the cruise control and I had reached all the way back behind the engine, to replace a small rubber hose. It was the small hose that made the cruise control operate. As I strained to attach the vacuum hose, it felt as though I had pulled every muscle from one end of my body to the other.

I immediately stood in an upright position, closed my eyes, and dropped into that perfect state of relaxation and told my body that everything was o.k.; that there were no torn muscles; that every muscle in my body was perfectly healthy; that every muscle was relaxed and healthy. I stood there and talked to my body for about one minute and then went on about my work. A few minutes later, I was able to reach in behind the motor and finish the work I needed to do, with no pain or strained muscles. Having had back problems in earlier years, I know that back problems are no fun. Again, I was really amazed that I had absolutely no soreness, no strain, and no pain.

Probably the most important time that I used hypnosis to protect myself was on a recent trip I took to Padre Island, along the Texas Gulf Coast. I always enjoy going to Padre Island because it is one of the last wildernesses left in the state of Texas. There is Spanish treasure on Padre Island from old shipwrecks, dating back to the 15th century. In 1965, I was lucky enough to find some coins from that treasure, and now you can see why I enjoy going back.

I was on Padre Island in my old 4-wheel drive Dodge Power Wagon, and the Power played out. To explain this story, let me back up a few days. We were doing quite well, until we drove out of our driveway in San Antonio, on our way to the Coast. As we drove into the street, we hit a low-hanging tree limb and ripped out one of the windows on the right side of our cabover camper. Well, that was o.k. We just put cardboard over the window, as a temporary measure.

We headed for the Island, which was about 150 miles from San Antonio. Along the way, we became aware that our Power Wagon was getting about five miles to the gallon. We discovered that the carburetor was not bolted down as tightly as it should be. We fixed that problem and that corrected the gas mileage.

We finally arrived on the Island, after spending $50.00 extra on gas, just to get there. I really pushed the old Power Wagon, in order to get down the Island. Padre Island is about 75 miles of nothing but fine-powered sand. The strain on the engine caused the engine to slip on the motor mounts. The engine then moved forward and the fan cut a hole in the radiator. When you are 50 miles from the nearest gas station, in the middle of sand dunes on one side and salt water on the other, it is very difficult to buy a can of radiator stop-leak. I remembered that some brands of radiator stop leak had tiny flakes of paper that would stop up the holes in the radiator. So, I called for a roll of toilet paper. I took several sheets of toilet paper, tore them into tiny pieces, and put them in the radiator. I added water and off we went. A few miles further, the truck started to overheat again. I loosened the radiator cap, so pressure would not build up in the radiator and blow the paper out of the holes. When we stopped to add water again, the radiator cap was still loose and there seemed to be no pressure in the radiator. For all of you fine mechanics out there, don't be fooled, like I was.

I removed the loose radiator cap, and the radiator exploded, spraying hot water, scalding water, all over my right arm! That's one of the worse kinds of burns you can get. The first thing I did was to drop into hypnosis, and again, I commanded my Subconscious the following: "There is no pain, no suffering; heal, heal." We had a can of burn spray in the emergency medicine box and I sprayed that on my arm and the pain got extremely intense. So, I went to the Power Wagon and sat down in the front seat. Again, I went into hypnosis for two or three minutes. I constantly commanded, "No pain, no suffering, no blisters." I even used the command that there were 500 needles of Novocain in my arm.

After two or three minutes, I got up from my hypnosis session with absolutely no pain, and in the waking state, I continued to command my body to heal. By the following day, maybe 20 hours later, I could take my hand and rub up and down on my arm and even pat the burn area, with no sensation. There were no blisters, no suffering, and no pain. There was only a deep, red birthmark-looking area where the water had hit my arm.

Three days later, the red area on my arm was still there and fading gradually. There was still absolutely no sign of burned or blistered tissue. I have seen people who have been burned by radiators exploding water on them and, believe me, it is not a pretty sight.

You have a Subconscious Mind. It controls your body functions. Use it!

NOTES

CHAPTER 35

INDUCTION PROCESS FOR POSITIVE INPUT

Now I am going to show you how to come face to face with the Subconscious Mind. When you give the Subconscious Mind direct commands, the results seem to be magical.

First of all, I want you to take a very relaxing position, preferably on an easy chair or on the bed. Do not cross your feet. Put your hands to your side. When going through this process, you will actually be talking to yourself. The Subconscious Mind should be talked to as though you are talking to a small child. When you give the commands, you must speak as though you are speaking to a child. The commands should be simple and to the point. For example, you give the command to relax; then you confirm the fact that you are relaxed. Such as, "Relax, relax all over my body. See there, I am relaxing. It feels good to relax."

You must tell the Subconscious Mind to do it. And then, confirm the fact, as though it has already happened. Keep in mind, the Subconscious Mind gives you exactly what you ask for, so anytime you say, "It is not working," the Subconscious Mind will say, "You are right. It is not working." But if you say to yourself, "I am relaxing," the Subconscious Mind tries to fulfill the command and you will actually feel yourself relaxing.

When going through the induction process, you should use a standard scale. Let's use the yardstick as a standard: thirty-six inches deep, thirty-six steps deep, or thirty-six paces deep. You will tell yourself that you will not go to thirty-seven. You must say, "Because at thirty-seven, it is a night-time sleep and I do not want to go into a night-time sleep, I will go only into a deep, relaxing sleep." (Understand that relaxed state is nothing more than a perfect state of concentration.) Then you say to yourself, "I will go down the scale one step at a time, until I am in a deep, relaxed sleep. Each step takes me deeper. I am relaxing more with each step." Then you begin to count down the scale.

Remember, as you are doing this exercise in your mind, you are actually talking to yourself in your mind. In between each step, you will give yourself commands. The commands do not have to be in any particular order. Say the numbers, in the following manner.

"One: I am going into a deep, relaxing sleep. I am going down a staircase that has 36 steps and each step takes me deeper, and I get more relaxed with each step.

Two: I will not go to step 37, because 37 is a sound sleep and I only want to go into a deep, relaxing sleep. I will go into a deep, relaxing sleep and I will be in a deep, relaxed state when I get to step 36.

Three: My body is more relaxed with each step. I am going deeper with each step. Each step takes me deeper and deeper.

Four: See there, I am getting deeper and I feel deeper. (You must confirm what you have said to your Subconscious.)

Five: Each number is more difficult to say than the last number. The numbers are getting so hard to say. When I can no longer say the numbers, I will be in a deep, deep, deep, relaxed sleep.

Six: See there, the numbers are getting harder to say.

Seven: The numbers are hard to say.

Eight: I am getting more relaxed with each number.

Induction Process For Positive Input

The numbers are taking me deeper and deeper and deeper.

Nine: Anytime I need to wake up in the case of an emergency, I will simply open my eyes and I will be wide-awake and I will have a clear mind. I will feel refreshed and I will feel as though I have slept for two hours.

Ten: The numbers are getting harder and harder to say, because I am getting more relaxed and more relaxed, with each number.

Eleven: Next time I relax myself, I will go deeper and faster, and very soon, I will be able to go into a deep, relaxed sleep with simply a thought or a word command."

The process will continue down the scale until you reach a point when a number can be said no longer, or you feel you are as deep as you need to be. What has happened is you have told your Subconscious Mind the way it is to be, and it has produced the conditions. You told your Subconscious Mind that the numbers would become hard to say. Your Subconscious is designed to protect you. Therefore, when the numbers get too hard to say, you will be in a deep, deep, relaxing sleep. (This is a state of perfect concentration.)

Before you go into your relaxed sleep, you need to have your battle plan made out, concerning the suggestions you want to give yourself. Plus, you will also tell yourself, as you go down the scale, "I will continue on the path to 36 before I fall into a sound sleep or before I wake up." If you do not program your Subconscious Mind to stay on the job, you will get so relaxed that you will drift off into a night-time sleep or a nap.

Deep relaxation is not sleep. It is somewhere between being awake and asleep. Some have called it an altered state of consciousness. Whatever the case, when you are in the super-relaxed state, you are more suggestible, and for some strange reason, the Subconscious Mind attempts to fulfill those suggestions. Remember that the Subconscious Mind gives you back exactly what you program, in the form of actions, feelings, and responses of some kind. These responses seem to be automatic after the programmed input. Also, suggestions given during this mental exercise, should also be suggested in the waking state.

Your mind works like a computer. Use it to your advantage. Stop all outside conditioning and condition yourself to respond as you would like.

All you are doing in the procedure I have described for you, is putting yourself into a deep, deep, relaxed state. When you go into this relaxed state, something happens in the mind. You are actually commanding your body to respond to your words.

You were designed to be in control of your mind and your own body. No one controls you, but you. When you are counting down the scale and putting yourself into that deep, relaxing state, the reason you tell yourself that the numbers are getting harder to say with each step, is to test the Subconscious to see if it is responding to your commands. The only reason that it would not respond to your command would be if you said or thought in your mind, "This is not working." Remember that the Subconscious gives you back exactly what you put in. Why would you say, "It is not working," while trying to relax yourself? You will be amazed when you first do this procedure. You will get very relaxed and the numbers will get harder to say, if you tell yourself that they are going to get harder to say.

Now that you understand basically how the Subconscious Mind works, you should use it to your

Induction Process For Positive Input

advantage. In the waking state, each and every thought, each and every word, each and every feeling, every sensation that you have, and every experience that you have is recorded in your Subconscious. Unfortunately, we have been trained in a primarily negative environment and the people around us think primarily negative thoughts.

In order to turn around our lives and make ourselves 100% healthy and 100% happy, we must simply change the way we think. An example: The client comes into my office and says, "I cannot change the way I think." First of all, he has made a negative statement, "I CANNOT." Secondly, he may not realize that he does his own thinking. He thinks only in the present and he cannot think in the past or in the future. You are to think only in the present. You can think *about* the past and *about* the future, but you only think *in* the present.

If I set an apple and an orange on the desk in front of you and ask you to think about which one you would like to have, you would do your own thinking and would select one or the other. So, if a man does his own thinking and he makes a statement that, "I cannot change the way I think," it is simply because he was trained to think he cannot. Also, if he says, "I cannot," in reality, he simply commands himself not to change. The next thing he might say is, "My wife and my job are killing me." Unless he has a definite need to be dead, why would a person say that his wife and his job are killing him? Negative phrases are all around us. The following is a list of phrases you probably hear everyday:

1. I worry myself sick.
2. I worry myself to death.
3. I cannot think straight.
4. My feet are killing me.

5. Aunt Sara is driving us crazy.
6. Just the thought of that makes me sick.
7. I am so tired I could die.
8. My boss is putting pressure on me.
9. I am under constant stress.
10. The world is going to hell in a handbasket.
11. I have to have a drink.
12. I cannot quit smoking.
13. I cannot break my bad habits.

The list goes on forever and ever and ever, unless we put a stop to it now. Be the first person in your life to take hold and decide to be happy and healthy and successful by simply thinking of yourself that way, and making the change this very moment.

From this day forward, condition your own mind. Do not allow the world to condition it for you. Choose to make the learning process positive and refuse all negatives. Put aside all antiquated theories as to what causes what, as far as your body is concerned, and control your body with your mind. Use your doctor as an aid, but YOU be responsible for your own good health.

You can be 100% positive. It's very simple. Command yourself: "I am a positive person that takes care of every situation in a positive manner. I am 100% relaxed, 100% calm, and 100% healthy. There may be certain situations that I like or dislike, but I simply choose to feel good all the time. I only use positive thoughts, and I only think in positive ways. I see the positive side of each and every situation. I see the other side of situations for my protection only."

You soon will find this will all come naturally, and you will feel healthier, happier, and stronger than you have ever felt before. This procedure has worked for countless others. Use it for your own lifelong happiness.

COMMENT FROM A CLIENT

Although I had been studying the laws of the mind and had made use of self-hypnosis, I had not been thoroughly successful. When I saw you, you pointed out several things, which I had been leaving out. I am very pleased to have found the key to becoming the person that I want to be now.

* * *

NOTES

CHAPTER 36
WHO IS TOM RAY?

Maybe I should tell you a little about how I became the "World's Greatest Hypnotist." I think it is very important to start in the beginning. However, in my case, I don't believe it is necessary to go as far back as Alex Haley did with *Roots*, so I will just say a few words about my Dad. In 1928, he was 18 years old and had been in an automobile wreck. As he lay on the emergency room table, the doctors felt there was no hope for him. I would not be here if he had not had the will to live, after the doctors told his family that he would be dead by morning and it would be a waste of time to take the piece of glass out of his neck. But when he was still alive by the next morning, they decided to operate. I learned of this story in my early teens. I didn't realize that half of his face was paralyzed. He always looked normal to me.

I was born in Joshua, Texas. Joshua is a little south of Ft. Worth. I have been there only twice; once to be born and once to see where it was. There is not a lot in Joshua, Texas. If you blink your eyes as you go through, you will miss it. Soon after my birth, we moved to Paris, Texas. My dad taught high school chemistry and also delivered ice to the German Prisoner of War camp in Paris.

They say every little rose needs fertilizing, so it will grow beautiful and healthy. That's what happened to me when I was about two years old! I don't recall anything about it. Maybe my Subconscious has blocked it out. Mother said that I fell through one of the holes in the outhouse in our backyard. She said that I didn't come out smelling like a rose! I don't know if that incident changed my life any, but many different things have happened to me.

I remember going to school barefoot in the snow. I didn't like to wear shoes and it was the first snow of the winter. Before leaving the house, I took off my shoes. When I got there, the teacher noticed that I had a great big coat on, but no shoes. They wanted to take up a collection to buy poor little Tommy Ray some shoes. At that time, I was not poor and I was not rich. My shoes were home under the bed.

My first grade teacher was also my father's first grade teacher. Her name was Mrs. Roundtree She must have taught school for about 50 years.

We moved from Paris, Texas to Magnolia, Arkansas, where my father taught at what was then known as Arkansas A&M College. Later, it became Southern State University and now I think it has another name.

The next major event in my life included one of the College faculty wives. She was supervising a swimming party at the water tank (pond) in the field behind the faculty homes. When it was time to go home, I was on an innertube and didn't want to leave. I was about 7 years old and didn't know how to swim. That is why I had the innertube. The lady called for everybody to get out of the water. Everybody got out, but me. She started toward the houses and I was still on the innertube in the water. Somehow, I fell off of it. The water was about 5 feet deep and I was only 4 feet tall. And obviously, that was too much water for such a little boy. I went under for the last time and I think I drank about half of the pond. Appearing on the bank was a young man that lived across the railroad tracks. He waded into the water. On him, it was only chest high. He took me by the hand and dragged me out of the water.

The next time I accidentally attempted to do myself in, was on a bicycle. I was riding down the middle of the street with my feet up on the handlebars. I must have been about 9 years old. They tell me my head made a very large dent in the front fender of a truck. It knocked me out completely and I woke up on the x-ray table in Dr. Wilson's clinic.

Dad taught us that if we started working at an early age, we would be more independent, we would have more spending money and would learn more about life. And like many young people, I thought my father was the smartest man alive.

There were many opportunities to find work. When I was 9 or 10 years old, I sold peanuts at the College football and basketball games. I got a cardboard box, put a rope on the box, strung the rope over my shoulders, so it would be easy to carry, and I was in business. I bought the peanuts from Mr. and Mrs. Peace who were in charge of the College bookstore and concession stands. I paid 8 cents for a sack of peanuts and sold it for 10 cents. There were some games where I could make $10.00 a night, which is 500 sacks of peanuts! That is a lot of peanuts and a lot of money for a 10 year-old boy, around 1949. When I was 11, I started delivering papers to the dormitories at the College. Our house was across the street from the College. The first paper I ever delivered was the *Arkansas Democrat*. The *Democrat* was the afternoon paper, so I delivered the papers after school. Then, I started delivering the *Daily Banner News*, which was the local daily paper in Magnolia, Arkansas. The *Daily Banner News* had to be delivered in the afternoon also, so I gave up delivering the *Arkansas Democrat*. I knew that I could make more money delivering the local paper.

A morning janitorial job came open at the local department store. The working hours were from 7 a.m. to 8 a.m. and involved sweeping out the store, before I went to school. I received a dollar for that hour's work, which was a lot of money, at that time. I had the morning job at the store and I delivered the papers for the *Daily Banner* in the afternoon.

I decided I could make even more money if I took a job selling tickets at the movies at night. Mr. W. P. Florence gave me a job at the Rocket Drive-In Theater. I would take the money from the person in the car, deliver it to the ticket counter, and return to the car, which was a distance of about 5 feet. It cost 45 cents for an adult to get into the movie and, generally, there were two people in the car. Most people paid with a dollar bill, so their change would be 10 cents. A box of popcorn cost 10 cents, so I convinced Mr. Florence to put a popcorn machine at the ticket counter. That way, when people gave me a dollar, resulting in a dime in change, I would ask them if they would like a box of popcorn, instead of their change. I sold about five times more popcorn than the boys at the concession stand did.

We moved from Magnolia, Arkansas to Odessa, Texas and it's probably a good thing. If I had stayed in Magnolia, I would probably been married at an early age, to a beautiful young lady named Peggy Jean. Not only was she the first girl I ever kissed, but she was the only girl I dated while in high school in Magnolia. She will always remain a special person to me. I wonder where she is today. I hope she is happy and healthy.

We moved to Odessa, Texas, where my father got a teaching position at Odessa College. That was back when Odessa had only one high school. Shortly after I enrolled in

Odessa High School, a student from the school's newspaper came to my homeroom and asked to speak with me. She said I was the 2000th student to enroll at that school and she wanted to write an article about me. At the end of the interview, she asked me, "Well, how do you feel?" and for some strange reason, I responded, "I don't feel any different than I did an hour ago." She printed that exact answer.

All throughout high school, I worked at different kinds of jobs. I also played drums in the band. My father would not allow me to play contact sports, because he had been a coach in his early days of teaching and he did not want me to get hurt. So, I was in the band. I always had pocket money, because I always worked. I think I had charge accounts at every store in town by the time I was 15 years old.

While in high school, I went swimming in an alum pond. Alum is the same stuff that is in a green persimmon. It makes your mouth pucker up. I went with a friend, Joe Walthal, and the reason we went to this particular pond to swim was because it was crystal clear. Apparently, vegetation and plant life do not grow in alum water. Joe and I swam across the pond. I was not the best swimmer in the world. We made it over, but I had trouble making it back. Joe was an excellent swimmer, and he had gotten all the way back across the pond and I was in the middle, trying to drown again. Well, the Good Lord decided he did not want to take me at that time and Joe dragged me out of the pond. By this time, it was my third attempt to accidentally do myself in and I figured I was being kept alive for some good reason.

As time went by, my father took the position as head of the chemistry department at Sul Ross State College in Alpine, Texas. I was a senior in high school. When it came time to select a Queen for the Fall Festival, I was dating a young lady that wanted to be Queen. Her name was Janith and, I think, bless ol' Janith's heart, that I helped get her elected. I had lots of friends in that small high school. She got elected and then she decided not to select me as her escort. She told me that I had not lived in Alpine all my life and it would be against tradition to select me. In the weeks before the coronation, she delayed her decision as to whom she would select. As a result of her delay, all the other boys were chosen for other positions. And guess who was the only boy left? Good ol' Tom Ray, and she had to select me. Boy, did I bask in my glory!

When I graduated from Alpine High School, I left Alpine, and went to college in New Mexico at the State University in Las Cruces. At the time I enrolled, it was called New Mexico A&M. Being an industrious young man, my room in the dorm was not on the average. I made trips around to all the junkyards and used furniture stores and with my ability to trade, buy, and sell, I had wall-to-wall carpeting, which was unusual for dorm rooms in those days. My room also had indirect lighting, a full-length dressing mirror, a hanging-ivy plant and a framed picture of a beautiful, yet tasteful nude. When it came time to have our rooms inspected, the Dorm Proctor did not even walk into my room. He just stood at the door, in amazement, and gave me an automatic AA+. The room next door always got an FF-!

Probably one of the reasons that my room looked so good was because the majority of the rooms looked so bad. The room next door that received the double F always was a disaster. One of the students was from Tennessee and the other was from Odessa. Between the two of them, they had about four clotheslines, a saddle, boxes of clothes, automobile parts, books, and a whiskey still! The whiskey still was the chemistry lab type, very compact, made from parts they had stolen from the chemistry lab. It was designed so that they could take a cardboard box and put over the still and no one would know the difference, especially with the rest of the junk in the room. The still sat right on the desk; that is how small it was, and they used it to make "white lightning."

There was a cage that housed their pet tarantula beside the still. There were many times we had to go on fly-catching trips to feed their tarantula. Then, there would be the times they would catch black widow spiders and put them in with the tarantula to see who would win. I don't think I was ever around to see one of those fights take place.

Probably one of the more memorable events of that year was the time the dead horse's head, with a little meat and a little hair still on it, floated from room to room. A group of us from my dorm had gone into the hills one weekend to camp. We brought back the horse's head. We had it on a piece of wire and we would hang it on someone's doorknob, hoping they would dispose of it. For some reason, it always wound up back in the junk room next door.

Before the spring break, the guys next door decided to box up the horse's head and sent it through the mail to another student's home. The best I can recall, that student's name was Chuck, from San Antonio, Texas. They supposedly marked the box, "DO NOT OPEN UNTIL EASTER." So, his mother did not open the box until Chuck got home. And, there was the horse head, stinky smelling, with a little less hair and a little less meat on it. After Chuck opened the box and saw that horse head, obviously he chose to bring it all the way back to New Mexico, and that horse head started around again. For a horse that had no body or legs, that was the fastest horse I ever saw!

The next time the Good Lord was looking out for me was in the same year, when we all went out to the abandoned airport behind the college to watch fireworks. Some of the co-op students that worked at White Sands Missile Range had stolen some solid jet propulsion rocket fuel. This fuel looked like pressed cow feed in the form of small bricks. These bricks came in varying lengths. One of the students found a metal box approximately one-foot square. He made a one inch thick steel plate lid for the box and bolted the lid on the box with about fifty bolts all around the lid. The lid had about a three-inch hole that you could stick the jet fuel into. The object was to stick the rocket fuel into the box, light the fuel and watch the fire come out of the hole.

There were about 50 students there that night to watch the fireworks. The lighting was to take place about midnight. The students stood on a hill about 50 yards from the box and one student went forward to light the fuel. As I recall, flames shot in the air about 30 feet! The box turned over on its side, with flames blowing straight toward the students. There was such a thrust, the box dug a one foot deep and ten feet long trench in the dirt. At that point, a piece of fuel inside the box blocked the hole and the box exploded! Those fifty bolts sheared off like they were made of Silly Putty and that one-inch thick steel lid went flying through the air and landed in the middle of the students. Miraculously, it did not hit a single person. If that steel lid had hit anyone, it would have cut him in half. So, if you are reading this and you work at White Sands Missile Range and you are a student, not trained to work with rocket fuel, you had better leave that rocket fuel alone.

I continued through college, finishing my education with a degree in general business and minors in chemistry and art. The only reason I had so much chemistry was that my father insisted on it. Remember, he was a chemistry professor. I took a couple of chemistry courses from him. To show you what type of fellow he was, he was looking out for me, so he gave me a D in chemistry and told me to try something else!

After I got out of college, I did not want to go to work. My Dad had programmed my Subconscious Mind. He used to say, "Son, go to college and get yourself a degree, so you don't have to work for a living." So, sure enough, like many other students who heard that message, I got my degree and I did not want to work. Again, you can see that you must be very careful of the words you use and the way you think, because the Subconscious Mind takes the words literally.

After I got my degree, I could not keep a job, because I really did not want one. I decided I would be better off, if I had an advanced degree. So, I worked on an advanced degree. At this point in time, I could have been classified as a professional student. I had all this information and I did not want to work. I figured I was too smart to work.

Back in the '60's, after graduation from college, Uncle Sam was breathing down my neck. I decided rather than getting drafted and being a foot soldier, I had better try to get a commission in the Air Force. I applied to Officer Training School.

At that time, I was living in Odessa, Texas and driving a Halliburton Cement Truck. (It's great to be a college graduate and be qualified to drive a truck.) We would drive out to the oil rigs where they were drilling and when the well was ready, I used my truck pumping equipment to pump cement down around the tubing to cement the pipe in the hole.

Probably one of the most unusual sights I have ever seen appeared one morning as I was driving my pump truck through the sand hills out from Crane, Texas. It was about 7 a.m. and the sun was just coming up. It was misting and raining just a little bit. Off in the distance sat a pump jack that was pumping oil out of the ground, right on top of a sand hill. A pump jack looks like a big, long-necked bird with its beak down in the ground. The sun broke through the clouds and there appeared a beautiful rainbow across the sky. The rainbow touched down exactly on top of the pump jack. Now there's proof that there is gold at the end of the rainbow. In this case, it was black gold.

When I got the call from the Air Force, I was still living in Odessa, Texas. I was going to have to give up my house, so I traded the equity in my house for the equity in a house trailer. It's important to tell you the size of the trailer. The trailer I traded for was 45 feet long by 8 feet wide. I decided it could cost too much money to have that house trailer moved to San Antonio by tow truck, so I bought myself a two-door Ford Fairlane 500 sedan to pull the trailer myself and save all that money. I went to a pawnshop and bought a set of overload springs that looked as if they had been made for a tank. I put them on that Ford and devised a mirror that stuck out about four feet on the driver's side of the car. I also purchased an electric brake switch that would engage the trailer brakes. I hooked up the Ford to the trailer and off I went to San Antonio.

Things were going pretty well, until I got to Junction,

Texas. On the east side of Junction, there is a hill bigger than you would ever believe. This hill had to be at least a good 80 degrees incline over a space of about three miles. The only problem was that the hill started right at a bridge and the bridge was right at the edge of the town. So, in order to get over that hill, I had to take a running start at the bridge and hopefully, make it all the way to the top. That Ford had an automatic transmission and I figured that with a good running start, I could go halfway up the hill in drive. Then, I could go over the top in low drive. Actually, it didn't work that way. I took a running start at the hill. About one-third of the way up, it appeared as though I would have to drop into low drive sooner than I had planned. As I began to slow down, I dropped into low, made it two-thirds of the way up the hill, and that's where I thought I was out of gears. The car pulling that big house trailer started going slower and slower. I swear I don't know what happened, but that Ford automatically dropped into a lower gear on its own and pulled that trailer over that hill, like a tank. To this day, I have not figured out what happened that caused the car to drop into a lower gear, especially when I had no more lower gears showing on the steering column. I made it all the way to San Antonio without one incident. And that was unusual for me.

After arriving in San Antonio and locating a nice trailer park, it was time to find a job. I was not scheduled to go into the service for a few more months. I convinced a small grocery store chain to hire me as an assistant accountant. I knew absolutely nothing about accounting, even though I had two accounting courses in college. If I remember correctly, my grades were C and D in accounting. However, I convinced a company to hire me as an assistant accountant. I worked for them for about four months, until it was time to go into Officer Training School at Lackland Air Force Base, Texas.

For anyone applying for OTS in Uncle Sam's Air Force, it is not what it is cracked up to be. About all you will get from OTS is your commission. Actually OTS might be considered to be an overgrown Boy Scout camp. I spent some time in the Scouts. I also grew up in an environment where we got to do all the things the Boy Scouts did and more. So, OTS was quite a breeze.

I remember one time when we went through the obstacle course. We had to climb on a rope that slanted down and across the river. (River? A glorified mud hole.) Almost every cadet fell in the river. Most of them had never been on a rope, especially going downhill backwards and about twenty feet over water. This rope reminded me of the rope we used to have running from one treehouse to another treehouse. So, I got on the rope, started down it backwards, and having flashbacks of younger days, I decided to go down using my legs only. I turned loose of the rope with my hands and hooked my legs on the rope, so there was no way I could fall. Then, I proceeded to walk down the rope upside down!

I knew that getting through OTS was going to be a snap, especially if I could keep my mouth shut. I found it difficult, however, to bite my tongue when I saw some of the things that happened while I was in OTS.

We were supposed to keep our rooms spotless, our shoes shined, and our beds made. That was pretty simple, because I did not live in my room. I shined my shoes once and put them under my bed where they belonged. I bought an extra pair of shoes and kept them in the empty room next door. In fact, I lived in the empty room next door and I don't think I made my bed twice the whole three months that I was there. It seemed foolish to go through the routine of making a perfect bed every morning and then messing it up to sleep in at night. I decided it would be much simpler to live next door in the empty room and to hide a complete set of everything I needed.

When I got up each morning, I would take my extra gear and put it under the drawer of the cabinet and close the drawer. If anyone came in and pulled out the drawer, all they would see was an empty drawer.

While I was at OTS, I had to learn to shoot a pistol. I had never held a .45 automatic in my hand before. My Dad always said to listen and do exactly what I was told. When I went to the pistol range, I listened and did exactly what I was told and I soon realized that I was a better shot than anybody was in my class. In fact, they made me the captain of the pistol team. To this day, I can shoot the eye out of a fly at 50 yards with a .45 automatic.

I received my commission at the end of my 90 days and volunteered for duty there at Lackland AFB. The only reason I volunteered for duty at Lackland was because I had that 45-foot house trailer and I did not want to move it again. All of the guys who didn't volunteer for Lackland got really nice overseas assignments.

While at Lackland, I had several jobs. I was a training officer for a time, at a Basic Training Squadron and another time, I was an administration officer. I worked in the Legal Office and at Wilford Hall Hospital, finally progressing to Assistant Chief Administrative Services at the Base Headquarters. I found, as a young Lt. in the Air Force, that if you acted as though you did not know anything and you couldn't scratch your backside with a handful of fishhooks, the Air Force would take care of you. But I felt the need to actually do something. That often created problems for me. While working at the headquarters office as the Assistant Chief of Administration of the Base, the Colonel I worked for wanted me to do a staff study on who should take the USAF Effective Writing Course. The Air Force came out with a regulation on who should and who should not take this course. The Colonel wanted the names of every Senior NCO and every officer on Lackland that was supposed to take the Effective Writing Course, according to the specs in the regulation. The particular Colonel I worked for must have thought if the Air Force could upgrade the ability of its senior officers to write and use Air Force terms properly, the paperwork would flow more smoothly. I can tell you now that staff study was the finest staff study ever written. There was only one problem. The very first name on the list, according to the regulations that I had researched, was the Base General. Following the Base General was a list of about 80% of the General's staff. Then about 75% of the Basic Training Squadron's officers. Obviously, the Colonel did not want to walk into the General's office and tell him that he did not know how to write effectively. The Colonel became very upset upon reading my study. I gave it to him and told him that, according to regulations, the Base General needed to learn to write more effectively. Probably some Senior NCO who had been in the service for thirty years worked up that regulation and that was his way of getting back at the hierarchy of the Air Force. Obviously, soon after that, the effective writing course died a horrible death at Lackland Air Force Base, Texas.

    The Colonel that I worked for was not at all happy with me. The final straw, as far as he was concerned, came one day when I really bucked the ol' Colonel and said, "NO!" Well, you can guess what happened from there. He proceeded to invite me to leave the Air Force. I left the USAF on a letter that was written under the regulation: "Convenience to the Air Force with an Honorable Discharge." What they did not realize was that it was more of a convenience for me to be out of the Air Force than it was for me to be in. Even though I had done probably five times more for Lackland AFB than any other First Lieutenant, I was simply asked to leave. During my time there, I met several nice officers. Unfortunately, a lot of officers felt they had to hold themselves to the system and I guess we can be thankful that the system does work. I felt that the whole Air Force could be run with about one-third of the people they had on duty. The finest officer I met was the Base Executive Officer and his name was Col. James Gunn. In fact Col. Gunn should have been the Base General. He would have made a good General.

I think you will remember in the television serial, "Black Sheep Squadron," the tough guy that is hard to control is the guy that generally outperforms the average man 3 to 1. So, if you have a person that is hard to control in your organization, find the key to that person and you will have an employee that will give you the work of three men.

After getting out of the Air Force, I went to work in a small meat packing company. While working for the company, I realized how really inefficient it was. I worked there for about three weeks and I couldn't keep my mouth shut any longer, so I decided to make a proposal to refine the system. Obviously, even with four years of college and three years of the military, I was still eager to change the world. I made my proposal to the owner of the meat packing company and he made me a proposal. He proposed that I look for another job.

The next job I stumbled onto was that of a medical supply salesman. I sold medical supplies to hospitals, nursing homes, and clinics. I spent eight years of my life going from hospital to hospital, and during that eight years, I learned absolutely nothing about the game of selling. After eight years of suggesting to the hospital supply firm I worked for how inefficient they were, they decided that it was not necessary that I work for them any longer. Even though, during the eight years that I worked for this company, I designed several new products, received one medical patent, won one sales contest to the Bahamas, and received a cash award for the best salesmanship "Article of the Year" in the Medical Supply Salesman Magazine. In spite of all this, I was asked to leave!

The basic problem I had in those days was that I passed on my ideas to others and they did not want to listen until I proved to them that I was the #1 Salesman. I am going to say to all of you Sales Managers in the world today: "If you only listen to your senior salesmen and you only listen to your #1 salesmen, you are making a serious mistake. You don't have to implement the ideas, but you should listen to all suggestions."

I went from selling medical supplies to selling burglar alarms. I convinced the president of a small burglar alarm company that I should be the Director of Marketing. With three employees in the company, it was foolish to have a Director of Marketing, but I visualized this small company turning into an IBM overnight, and, believe me, that is not the way it works. I met one of the best friends I ever had while I worked for this company. I left the burglar alarm company when the president made me a proposal to find another job.

I next went to work for a while selling industrial chemicals. That is a fancy name for janitor supplies. I am going to say now to all the sales managers, if you want a good salesman, hire yourself a good ex-chemical salesman. I spent three years selling chemicals and I learned more about selling in those three years than in anything else I have ever done. I learned more about how to maneuver the buyer than I thought was ever possible. I believe that was the most interesting job in selling I ever had.

Before the chemical company asked me to look for another job, I suggested one day to the president how to increase his sales by about three quarters of a million dollars a year. By simply a small expenditure of $7.00 per salesman, he could have increased his sales enormously. Again, I was told that I was not the #1 salesman of the company and when I became #1, they would consider my suggestions. I think, at this point, there is a story that is applicable.

Once upon a time, there was a truck driver who drove under a bridge and his truck was too tall to get through the underpass. All the engineers from the trucking company and the highway department came out and tried to figure out how to get the truck unstuck. They could not solve the problem. Then, a small boy riding his bicycle came by and said to the driver, "I know how to get your truck out from under the bridge." The truck driver, not being one burdened with a management complex, asked the boy how to do it. The young boy said, "Let a little of the air out of the tires." They did and it worked.

About five years ago, this same incident happened to me in San Marcos, Texas. I wasn't a young boy, but I told the truck driver to let some air out of the tires. He did, and he drove it right out.

While selling for the chemical company, I found it quite easy to go to work on Thursday at noon and work all afternoon and half a day on Friday, and I was able to sell enough chemicals to stay up with the rest of the fellows. During that time, the friend from the burglar alarm company suggested that we go into the nightclub business.

I had visions of being like Hugh Hefner, starting my own chain of nightclubs, with beautiful women working for me. Even though I was a non-drinker, and had not drunk more than a half dozen drinks my entire life, I decided to go into the nightclub business with my friend.

San Antonio is not as big a city as some are, so I figured that if I copied the Playboy Bunny uniform and changed it a little, Hugh Hefner would not be on my case. I changed the ears and used a maid's cap- kind of a little lace affair. Instead of white cuffs and a bow tie, I used a velvet choker and lace cuffs. I designed a lace apron, to complete the outfit.

With the uniforms designed, we were ready to interview for positions. Our first mistake was not following up on references after we interviewed the girls and made our selections. The second mistake was that we paid them too much money to wear those fancy uniforms. But, when we opened the doors for business, we looked as though we knew what we were doing. In those uniforms, our waitresses were some of the most beautiful women I have ever seen. However, we learned (after I got out of the nightclub business, three months and $10,000 in debt later), that the young ladies we had hired were not what they seemed to be. Even though each looked like the girl next door, one had spent six years in a federal pen; one was an 18 year old that got pregnant; one was so good-looking that all the men would not leave her alone and she quit the second day; and the last one was your average girl next door, wife and mother, who decided, after a couple of months of working in the club, that she would leave her family and go on the nightclub circuit!

One of the reasons I didn't make it in the nightclub business is that my business partner and I didn't agree on how to run the club. We would sit in the back room and, while the jukebox was playing, we would scream and argue. When the jukebox stopped to change records, we would stop arguing. I hope the people in the club never heard us, but it doesn't matter now.

I relinquished my half of the business to him and took the blood bath for $10,000. I know, to a lot of people, this amount of money is not a lot, but to a small town boy without a lot of money, that was a goodly sum. I was still selling chemicals, while I owned the nightclub and, basically, what I was trying to do was to be an absentee owner. That does not work in the nightclub business.

About the time I was losing all my money, I lived in a trailer house behind the club. I was divorced at the time and I had gotten very short of money. I had failed to pay the mortgage payment for the house trailer for several months. One day, I came home from a road trip of selling chemicals and when I drove up to the lot where my home was supposed to be, there was nothing there. Just the steps leading up to nothing. Somebody had stolen my trailer. Later, I found out that the banker had my trailer and he wanted his money for the back payments. I had known this banker for about 15 years and I considered him to be a good friend. On that day,

I think he taught me a lesson. To this day, he is still a good friend. His name is Jim Law, one of the finest, toughest men I know. I really respect the man. I had always had A-1 credit before the nightclub business. Things changed drastically in my credit department. And, believe me, once you ever lose your credit, it takes years and years to get it back.

Soon after I lost $10,000 in the night club business, I decided to do something with my inventions. I have always been the inventive type. I was trained to look for a better way of doing things. I decided to take a puzzle that my friend, Tom Posey, and I designed and have some finished prototypes made. I designed a box and a display case and off I went to the New York Toy Fair.

I went to the New York Toy Show to see how the big boys did it. There I was, a small town boy in New York City, learning how to present a product at a toy convention. I already was an expert on conventions, because of attending all those medical supplies conventions in the past. (I guess I did learn a little something while I was selling those medical supplies.) I believe all conventions are probably about the same. The only difference between one convention and another is the products that are being presented. I went to New York and learned a lot; came home and made preparations to display our new product at the Dallas Toy Fair. I designed the booth and made all the display materials by hand. When I finished and had the booth all set up, I looked as suave and professional as Parker Brothers or Mattel. I was just a young man with stars in my eyes and a lot of guts!

I took my product to the Toy Fair and there was only one problem: I got so many orders that I closed my company and never delivered one unit. A banker had told me that if I went to the show and brought back orders, his bank would loan me the money to float my project and my company. After I went through all this creativity, the designs, the conventions and the orders, the banker told me that he could not get the board to approve the loan. I would just have to wait until I had the money to produce the product myself. To this day, the product is still in the closet.

While at the Toy Fair, I was able to set up lines of distribution, so that I had all markets available to me. I had support in all quadrants of the U.S., ready to sell whenever the product was ready. But, surprise, surprise, no money. I hope to take part of the money that you paid for this book and float the many projects that I have. There are several unique products that I have designed. Some of them are in the field of surgery, general medical supplies, wearing apparel, such as jewelry, and some in the energy field. One, obviously, is that secret puzzle in the closet.

It is very easy to be creative. But just being creative is not enough. You must create and follow through. I will use the money from this book to promote other things I want to do. So, be sure to tell your friends to buy a copy of this book. We are extremely fortunate that in America, free enterprise still exists; but because of some of our politicians, it may not exist for long. We must take care of ourselves today and plan for the future. If you are sitting around doing nothing with that really exciting product you have designed, get it out of the closet and start pushing. Keep pushing and pushing until somebody, somewhere, buys your idea.

If you say to yourself, "I can't make it," the Subconscious Mind says, "You are right. You cannot." And, if you say to yourself over and over again, "I can make it. Do something today. Do it right now," the Subconscious Mind says, "You are right. You can do it now." Then the Subconscious will make you produce. So, never say die. When you get knocked down, get up. When you get shoved down, get up. When you get stomped on, get up. You always have the ability to get up. If you do not get up, it is purely your choice. You control your own destiny. You control your own feelings, thoughts and words. You simply say to yourself, "I never give up. I always make it because I am #1." You use all the positives that you can think of. By just saying the words, the Subconscious Mind will make you produce. You are designed that way.

Throughout my life, at least for the last twenty years, I have collected, bought and sold just about everything you can think of. One day, I got very interested in buying, selling, and collecting books. Strangely enough, I made it through college and through graduate school without reading one book in its entirety. I would read parts of books, but I never read one book from cover to cover until after I got out of graduate school. I am not proud of the fact, but growing up, I was taught to be a poor reader, even though both of my parents were fine teachers. They always said, "Tommy is a poor reader," so I did what I was told.

One day, while I was buying and selling, I decided to specialize in fine and rare books. All of a sudden, books became very fascinating to me. A book is a representation of an individual's thoughts. I have always been interested in the way people think and why they do the things they do. When I hold a book in my hand, it gives me permission to possibly see inside the author's mind. It helps me to understand how he may have thought. So, as I look at my collection of rare books, I do not look at the books as books. I look at the books as real people that have feelings, hopes, dreams, disappointments, happy times, etc. I now read books and I treasure each and every book that I have, because I know with that book, I can be very close to the person who wrote it. I am human like everyone else and I enjoy being with people.

One day, I picked up a hypnosis book. The title was *Hypnotism and its Application of Practical Medicine* by Otto Georg Wetterstrand, M.D. The book was dated 1902. Dr. Wetterstrand was a German physician that had used hypnosis in connection with his medicine. After I read through that book, I became fascinated with his work and with the art of hypnosis.

I started collecting everything I could get my hands on that had anything to do with hypnosis. Very few people knew this and very few people knew that I thought there was a lot to be gained in the field of hypnosis. After about ten years of study and observing everything that had anything to do with hypnosis, I became a self-taught hypnotist.

Now, I am the world's best hypnotist. The reason I am the world's best hypnotist is because I have programmed myself to be the world's best. As a result, I have developed techniques and procedures that the world of hypnotism thought never could be done. It is unimportant that you believe that I am the world's best. It is only important to me.

I think of myself as the world's best; I produce like the world's best; and I get results like the world's best. As a result, I AM the world's best. You must plant the good information in the Subconscious Mind first. If you do not command the mind, others will command it for you and you may become that brainwashed human being that does as he is told. Use what I teach as a guide. Understand the consequences, but control your own thoughts. Do not allow the world around you to control your life. Do your own conditioning. Why should you be like Pavlov's dogs? When the bell rings, you were taught to automatically react. By understanding your Subconscious and using it in your everyday life, you become 100% happy, 100% healthy, and 100% positive, regardless of how other people think or act. If you will use the ability that God or your Creator gave you, then you can be the person that you choose to be. If you choose anything other than being happy, being healthy, and being #1 with yourself, you must understand, it is simply your choice. You will get the rewards of your choice.

At this point in time, I have been a student of hypnosis for more than twenty years. I had an office in the South Texas Medical Center from 1977 to 1990.

I have lectured at different places around the world. I have worked with almost every major physical and psychological problem man can have, and I have seen changes take place that are almost unbelievable.

I have coached movie stars; professional singers; athletes, from grade school to the pro ranks; janitors to bank presidents; doctors; lawyers; and one guy that claimed to be an Indian chief!

The payoff was not the money I made. The payoff was the healthy changes I saw in the people I worked with. You, too, can be changed if you read, re-read, and use what I teach you in this book.

Since the first draft of this book, I am no longer a practicing professional hypnotist. You won't believe what I am up to these days. Stay tuned for Book #2!

CHAPTER 37

WHAT HAPPENED TO TOM RAY?
30 HOURS IN A DAY!
WHY DID TOM RAY CRASH?

This is the last and final chapter of this particular book. I want to share with you something that happened to me. I do not want you to do some of the no-good things that I did.

The date of the writing of this chapter is twenty years from the date of the first chapter. Several months ago, I was eating breakfast at one of the local restaurants. Something strange came over my body, almost instantly. I could not eat my breakfast. I began to shake or quiver inside my body and I had to get up from the table and go outside.

From that day forward, I had a total loss of appetite, but knew I had to eat to survive. I began to drink V8 juice, chocolate milk, or any other liquid that I could quickly put into my stomach. I could drink the juice or whatever my wife liquefied in the blender, but I could no longer face food on a plate. Once the juice or blended food was in my stomach, the jitters, gut nervousness, and/or "feel-bads" went away. In an hour or so, I had to drink something again, because the jitters reappeared.

Part of my continuing body breakdown was a result of my attempt to solve the situation. In other words, as I tried to find the answer to the body breakdown and was not able to, it created for me, a very big *yes/no* situation.

Remember, the mind cannot handle a yes/no situation and will send you a "feel-bad" in order to get you off the *yes/no* thinking and to get you to think *"yes"* or *"no"*.

Here I was, having these strange things happen in my body and I could not find the answer. At first, I thought I had food poisoning. I went through every scenario possible, but still I had the "feel-bads." I began to lose weight rapidly. I was deteriorating, both mentally and physically. Early in the process, I went to the doctor and he concluded, after about five minutes, that I had an over-acid stomach and I was depressed. I just laughed in his face. "Tom Ray depressed? Doc, you've got to be out of your mind!" He gave me pills for my stomach and pills for the depression and I went home and did not take them. My mistake.

Doctors are trained to assist us in returning to good health. You should listen, but not become totally dependent on the doctor. You and you alone are responsible for your good health. Your doctor is there to aid you and direct you. Use his advice, but do not become a "doctor junky," like a lot of people do. For the doctor junky, every little thing that comes up means a trip to the doctor.

Back to my story. I did not take the pills. I continued to self-analyze and, unfortunately, agonize over my inability to solve the lousy conditions I was experiencing inside my body.

As time went by, I talked as though I must be going crazy. I knew that I was not going crazy, because I knew I had control of my illogical Subconscious. That still did not stop me from verbalizing that "I must be going crazy." Since "I must be going crazy" is a command, my downward spiral continued. I experienced crazy thoughts. I tried to analyze the reason for the crazy thinking, and I came up with no answers. So, the *yes/no* situation kicked me in the face again.

Here I was, Tom Ray, super-genius, the man that wrote the *Laws of the Subconscious*; the man that taught and helped thousands; and I was beginning to realize that I was not solving my own health problem.

I knew all along I was not a Superman. I liked to play in my mind that I was Superman. I believed I could overcome any and all adversities. But, here I was, thinking crazy thoughts, and doing crazy things inside my body.

The downfall continued. As I analyzed the situation, I dragged up every mistake that I thought I had made throughout my life. As I dragged up these mistakes, my mind would send me another "feel-bad." The more "feel-bads" I had, the more I thought I was going crazy!

The more I thought I was going crazy, the more conflict I had in my mind. I knew full well that I consciously control my Subconscious. Therefore, I could not go crazy. But, I still had the hurt in my guts and nervousness in my body every hour or so, if I did not chug-a-lug some liquid nourishment. The pain and jittery feeling continued, so I kept going down the tubes, emotionally and physically.

I started going to every doctor I could find that I thought could help me. I first went to an Internal Medicine doctor who said I had acid reflux and I was depressed. He made this conclusion in about five minutes and I didn't take his advice.

The second was an Internal Medicine holistic health doctor. After all his tests and hundreds of dollars later, he concluded my body chemistry was perfect. He said I must be depressed. HA! Not that again.

The third doctor was yet another Internal Medicine doctor that prescribed a lot of vitamins and natural substances. He said I overworked myself and my adrenal glands were probably shot and, as a result, I was depressed.

By now, I could still find no real problem, but my body still hurt. I still had the jitters, and I was continuing to lose weight. With each encounter, the doctors said I was physically healthy; my blood chemistry was excellent; and, basically, I must be depressed and stressed. Again, I was not buying it. This added fuel to the fire of the *yes* and *no* together. I felt lousy. They said I was healthy. I could not conceive of myself as being depressed. Down the tubes, I continued.

I would wake between four and five o'clock in the morning, shaking and quivering inside. So, I would go to the kitchen and chug-a-lug orange juice and a thick protein drink that a friend suggested. I would go back to bed and about two hours later, the shakes would start again. Then, I would get up, go outside and walk very fast, up and down the steep driveway behind my house. I must have looked like a man possessed! By doing this crazy walking, I seemed to be able to tolerate the "feel-bads."

I went to my shop building earlier and earlier every day, taking snack items, such as cheese, fruit and crackers, to pick at all day long. I drank V8 juice and chocolate milk or whatever I could find that I thought would help me. Sometimes I would crawl around the floor in my house and cry. On bad days, which was almost every day, I would have both crying and self-analysis sessions with my wife. While I was doing all of these crazy things, I was attempting to analyze and rationalize each and every action. It was like being down a hole, shoveling out dirt, while some clown (me) was shoveling the dirt back in the hole.

I was obsessed with solving this craziness. After exploring these actions with one doctor, he prescribed pills for OCS, obsessive compulsive disorder. I had been pegged again. But, each crazy thing I did was nothing more than an attempt to stop the shaking and pain in my body.

Many weeks passed and I did nothing, except suffer the "feel-bads" and do crazy things. Now the pain in my body did not let up, so I began to think, "I'll just get rid of the pain by killing myself." I knew full well that I was not going to kill myself. I knew I had total control over my "feel-bad" thoughts from the Subconscious. The Subconscious is not logical, so it sends out different thoughts in ways to get rid of the "feel-bads."

I would get thoughts of drugs. I am not stupid. I don't take drugs. I thought of alcohol. Still, I am not stupid. I know alcohol will not solve the problem. It will only numb the brain and make you squirrelly in the process, plus, cook your liver.

I thought about electrocution, but I knew that could possibly only cook my brain and I would be a veggie. Plus, I knew I would not, at any time, do anything to harm my body. That did not keep me from talking to my wife about my thoughts. She related those conversations to my kids and they had her remove anything she thought I could kill myself with. I only wish she could have been inside my mind. I had no intention of ever hurting myself. I was trying to figure out how to help myself. Remember, all this time, I was trying to find answers. But, when my wife heard me talk of doing myself in, she became even more concerned.

I knew that I needed all the good suggestions I could get, in order to survive this ridiculous situation. During my better times, I made three special Tom Ray Tapes, to support my healing process. I used those three tapes, plus my standard Relaxation Tape and my Good Health Tape. I truly believe that without this mental support, I would be dead today. I knew I had a choice. I chose to live. When you are alive, you can eventually overcome adversity. When you are dead, you have no second chance.

All during this time, I would have moments of "feel-goods." During those times, I would instruct my wife on how she was to deal with me during my *crazy times*. I call them my *crazy times*, because my thinking was sometimes illogical. Those times were nothing more than the illogical Subconscious sending out suggestions on how to deal with the "feel-bads."

I must have called every friend I had, in an effort to find answers. I called a high school friend that is an RN, Ph.D. and asked for her advice. I followed it and, for a couple of days, I was fine; but then, I went back to "crazy feel-bad city." I called an old fishing buddy and told him I thought I was going crazy. I went to see him and had two good days and then back to "squirrel city."

I searched out anybody that I knew that may have encountered this type of situation and everybody generally concluded that I was overworked and depressed. HA! Not again! Not me, Tom Ray! I was Superman!

I decided I must be dying of heart trouble; therefore, big "feel-bad." So, I spent even more money and went to see a heart specialist. He put me on the treadmill, took pictures of my heart, and indicated I was as healthy as a horse. Bear in mind, I am now 60 and he said I was in super-dooper great health, heart-wise. When I was on the treadmill, he had to almost get me into a full run to get my heart rate up. That means I am so relaxed, I can work and walk and exert myself and still not get overly fatigued. You guessed it! The heart doctor concluded that I must be depressed.

I decided to go to another Internal Medicine

specialist, because that was where the pain and "feel-bad" was and he sent me to have an abdominal CT scan, which meant more money down the tubes. The scan basically found nothing. I was perfectly healthy. He convinced me that I should take the antacid pills; take the anti-depression pills; and also, take a little valium.

The internal mental conflict really began. What would happen to all those nice people that read my book and found out that I took anti-depression pills and valium. My goose was really cooked. The big *yes/no* gremlin was really about to get me.

I decided to do as he said. I started taking the acid pills and the depression pills to see if I would get a change in the abdominal pain. I seemed to get a little relief, but not total. My craziness continued until one day I felt so bad, crazy-wise that I decided if it were my time to die, even with all the projects I had on the table, so be it.

Fortunately, I was too healthy to die. I was just confused. During all this time, I had bouts with crying, sleeping all the time, and not eating: classic examples of severe *yes/no* thinking. As we all know by now, the doctors call that "depression."

One morning, I was having a really bad time and I was getting nowhere fast. The pain and misery had reached a level that had I been struck by lightening and died, my Subconscious would have won. Unfortunately, if you kill yourself, you cannot come back tomorrow and do all those fun things there are to do out there in this exciting world.

During that morning's crying and crazy talk, (Bless my wife's heart; she deserves a crown for putting up with me) I finally let everything go and turned it over to my Maker; my God. This allowed my mind to have peace. If you do not have a God and you allow yourself to get to where I was, read, re-read and read my book again; talk to some professionals; get some outside opinions. But, finally, change the way of life that got you to where you are. Let it go. Take another path. It doesn't hurt to get advice from others and to use that advice.

    Here is what happened to me. Remember, I thought I was Superman. I was in the process of running a small one-man business as an RV dealer. The reason I left the Hypnosis business was that when I went into the business, there were only 3 or 4 of us in town, and 10 years later, hypnotists were all over the place. If you have too many gas stations in town, someone is going to go broke. I went into the RV business, because it made me a living and I enjoyed doing it. I would sell 50-75 units a year.

    OK, here I was selling 50-75 RV's a year. I had to find them and then buy them. I had to get them home. I had to fix them, advertise them and then, show them to customers. Finally, I have to sell them and sometimes, even deliver them. All this involved one to two units a week, which was a lot of effort.

    During this time, I also obtained my third U.S. Government patent. I was working hard with one of my sons on a patent we have together, a really neat lighted name tag (www.glotag.com) and was attempting to build a large company with little money. I spent every moment of my time writing, working, and starting a company. Now, I decided I needed to build an office complex to house these offices we were going to need. Only I decided to build them myself, by hand! Yes, hammer and nails!

    My regular RV job, my patent promotions, my writing, my attempt to help everybody that needed help and money, my completion of this book, after 20 years, and, guess what? The body gave out. I would get fatigued, not eat, take aspirin for the pain of fatigue, and I became a work, no-play freak, needing 3 to 4 aspirins every night, which caused havoc with my system. I crashed one day and you know the rest.

My very simple suggestion for you is to live life in moderation. Understand you are not going to save the world. Understand that all those around you are not your responsibility, unless they are children or the elderly. Help when you can, but save a little piece of mind for yourself. Control that Subconscious, do a few good deeds and live a long, healthy and happy life. Remember to tell the truth, because the Subconscious cannot handle *yes* and *no* together.

I am now back to being my old self. My eating is back to normal. I have no pain and I am completely off the medicine. My health is completely restored. I no longer take on the problems of the world. I am not Superman. I am only the messenger. What you do with the message I give you is your doing, not mine. If you gain, fine. If you lose, it's not my fault.

I would like to make your world perfect, but I must keep myself healthy first. I must put myself first and stay healthy, in order to help teach you how to make your world perfect. Let yesterday go. You can start fresh everyday. Every moment is a fresh, new start.

My world is now perfect. I simple broke my own *Laws of the Subconscious* and suffered the result. Let this be a lesson to you. Don't go where I went. You may not come back. Thank God, I came back, and I mean that literally! The End! Heavens, no! This is just the beginning!

NOTES

CHAPTER 38

LETTERS...I GET LETTERS

Letters, I get letters. It seems like every time I give a speech or seminar or appear on TV or a radio talk show, I get letters. I am going to share a few of these letters with you, but for obvious reasons, am omitting the names.

LETTERS FROM MY NEWSPAPER COLUMN:
Ask the Hypnotist

Dear Tom Ray,

I have read that hypnosis can help people that have phobias of all kinds. My problem is that I have a fear of flying and a fear of high places. I am eighteen years old and I would like to be a commercial airline pilot or an astronaut.

Signed,
Junior Astronaut

Dear Junior Astronaut,

Your fear of flying and high places may go back to an uncomfortable incident in your life that was closely related to high places, or it may not even be related to high places or airplanes. The way to solve this problem would be to go back in your Memory Bank or Subconscious and find out when all this started and what the related or unrelated fears were at the time.

I had a similar case where a young pilot had

developed a fear of flying his private aircraft at high altitudes, but the fear did not exist while he flew his plane at low altitudes. We discussed all the events surrounding the few days before and the time he first experienced the problem.

It had happened like this: One day, he was flying at approximately fifteen thousand feet and he looked down at the ground and became very frightened and scared. He landed at the nearest airport, rested for a few hours and tried it again. As long as he flew low, he did not have this problem. This became very worrisome to him, because he could not always fly at low altitudes.

I asked the young pilot to go back in time and tell me when he first remembered having a similar fear. I waited for a few moments and he raised his finger, indicating that he was at the time and place where a similar fear existed. I asked him to remain calm and tell me exactly where he was and what was happening. He remembered that he had gone to a movie with his father and older brother to see a special science fiction feature and had become frightened at what he had seen. I could see no connection between the movie and the existing fear, and I asked him to tell me some of the things that he remembered about the movie. He mentioned several unreal-looking creatures and the presence of wavy lines and unusual shapes and lights, obviously created by the movie producers for effect.

After additional questioning and probing for answers, it was obvious that when the young pilot was flying at about 15,000 feet one day, he looked down at the ground and saw similar lines and shapes on the ground and it triggered the fear that he had experienced that day at the movie. He had become so frightened that his father and brother had to leave the movie with him, before it ended.

He later discussed the situation with his father. His father confirmed the fact that this situation did happen. When the pilot saw that his fears had nothing to do with flying itself, he overcame his fear of flying at high altitudes.

Dear Tom Ray,

I have a teenage son that until recently, was a very good student in school. During the last few weeks, his grades have dropped to nil and he has no interest in school. I have received calls from the school, telling me that he has been cutting class. On many days, he does not even show up at the school. Can hypnosis help my boy?

Signed,
Frustrated Parent

Dear Frustrated Parent,

I work with many children and it is very easy to locate problem areas and help children deal with existing situations in life, through the use of hypnosis.

Very often, young boys and every once in a while, a young girl will be harassed by a fellow schoolmate and the child will not tell his parents or the teachers. About seven out of ten that I see, below the age of 15, have that particular problem.

All you have to do is ask in a kind, point-blank manner, if someone is bothering him at school or on the way to school. A familiar situation in today's school society is the case of extortion, commonly called the protection racket.

One student will demand payment from another, using the threat of violence.

Usually the person that is doing the threatening is the child that is having the most problems. That student is usually absent a lot. That student is usually not living with his parents. That student is the person that generally needs the most help.

If your son will not talk to you about the situation, do not despair. A competent, reputable hypnotist will find it very easy to get the young man to give his gut feelings under hypnosis. At this time, when the situation is out in the open, you will be better able to deal with it in a satisfactory manner.

The one major point I will stress here is for the schools to develop programs to teach the students to have self-worth. Let's teach our children that they are somebody important. Let's teach them that they do not have to be sexually, physically, or emotionally abused. Let's teach them that they must be Number One with themselves. This would have a tremendous, positive effect on the system.

Dear Tom Ray,

I have been smoking for about 35 years and the other day, my doctor insisted that I stop smoking. He gave me the ultimatum that if I wanted to live much longer, I was going to have to quit smoking. I can go without the cigarettes for about 3 hours and then, I feel like I am going to die if I don't get a cigarette. I get nervous and jittery and I pick up the cigarettes again. Will hypnosis help?

Signed,
Nervous Smoker

Dear Nervous Smoker,

Smoking is not your problem. Smoking cannot relax you. It is the "thought" of smoking that relaxes you, momentarily. A perfectly relaxed and in-control person can put down his cigarettes and simply quit. If you allow your Subconscious to control you, however, you will never quit. If you take control of your Subconscious and tell it what to do, you will find it very easy to quit.

If you will follow these simple instructions, smoking will become a part of your past. And, as I have said in previous columns, the Past does not exist, so you might as well let bygones be bygones.

STOP SMOKING PROCEDURE:

Set aside about 5 minutes twice a day and take a comfortable position in an easy chair. It is very important to be in a quiet room. You might go through this procedure right before going to bed and again, right after waking up in the morning.

For about 30 seconds, repeat your first name and the word, "relax." Example: "Tom, relax. Tom, relax. Tom, relax. Tom, relax." If you are doing this exercise at night, every few moments you must tell yourself that you will not go to sleep until you have finished giving yourself the "no-smoking" instructions.

After you have relaxed yourself, repeat the following, "I no longer smoke and I am relaxed, not smoking." Repeat this statement about 5 to 10 times. During the day, if you feel like having a cigarette, say in your mind, the same statement: "I no longer smoke and I am relaxed, not smoking." This reinforces for the Subconscious Mind that you are a relaxed, healthy, happy non-smoker.

As you may remember from previous information that has been in this column, that feeling for a cigarette was not a feeling for a cigarette. It was an uncomfortable feeling, as a result of your seeing only the negative side of a situation. All that has changed now!

Dear Tom Ray,
　　Several months back, I read a newspaper article where you said you could cure a football player that had been paralyzed from the neck down. Either you are God or you are a quack.

　　　　　　　　　　　　　　Signed,
　　　　　　　　　　　　　　Mad Sports Fan

Dear Mad Sports Fan,
　　I am not God. I am not a doctor and I am not a quack. I heal no one. I can only heal myself. You have the same power. You, and only you, control your Subconscious and your Subconscious controls your body.
　　I can show an injured football player or anyone else how to control the body functions through the Subconscious, thereby returning to perfect health.
　　By the way, the term "quack" comes from a gentleman by the last name of Quack, who pretended to be a real Medical Doctor.

Dear Tom Ray,
　　My sister has cancer and the doctors are using "bio-

feedback" in her cancer therapy program. What is biofeedback and will it do her any good?

Signed,
Curious Sister

Dear Curious Sister,

To explain "biofeedback" in everyday language, I will tell you that during the biofeedback process, the subject learns to relax his or her body to the point that a change in minute electrical impulses from the body can be recorded on a machine. The object is to reduce the number of electrical impulses produced by the body, thereby producing relaxation. The reduction of electrical impulses is, then, the gauge.

Biofeedback has its advantages. The person can learn to relax and relaxation is the name of the game. When a person is totally relaxed, his chances of returning to perfect health are greatly increased.

However, it is not necessary to be hooked up to a biofeedback machine, in order to learn to relax. It would be a little ridiculous if everyone went around with little electrodes taped to their foreheads.

Total relaxation can be easily learned and achieved with hypnosis. The difference between biofeedback and hypnosis is that if you are going to go into this super-relaxed state, you might as well give commands to your body. When a person is in this relaxed, suggestible state and commands the body, as though the change has already happened, then the body makes the change and is able to achieve perfect health again, regardless of what the illness is. It has been proven time and time again, that we can control our body functions.

Dear Tom Ray,
    My sister lives in Los Angeles and has been going to a hypnotist to help her overcome her fear of driving. To me, it sounds foolish that she has a fear of driving, because when we were in college together, she used to do all of the driving when we would go somewhere. But, she had a minor automobile accident about 2 years ago and hasn't driven since. I have talked to her about it and pointed out that she has had accidents before, minor ones also, but now, she is afraid of driving. How is the hypnosis going to help her from being afraid?

Signed,
Concerned Sister

Dear Concerned Sister,
    As in all of my answers to questions such as this, I must say that I, personally, have not had the chance to probe her Subconscious to find the answer. It is very likely that she was being bothered by something else on the day that she had the accident, and her fear of driving may be the Subconscious Mind's way of warning her that the same uncomfortable conditions or the thoughts of the uncomfortable situation will arise.
    I had a similar case in my office. A young lady, in her 20's, came to me because of a fear of driving. She was engaged to a young Air Force helicopter pilot. A few days

before she was involved in a minor car accident, she had heard that her betrothed was reported "missing in action." We discussed her driving and the accident and all the things that had happened around the time of the accident. During our discussion, she never mentioned the situation with her fiancée. However, once we started into the hypnosis, it was soon apparent that there was no real associated reason for her fear of driving. When she understood this, her fear of driving soon faded. Through the aid of hypnosis, she learned not to worry about something that she could do nothing about, even she loved her fiancée very much and was hopeful for his safety.

Dear Tom Ray,

    I would like to know if hypnosis can cure a person from talking in his sleep. About 6 months ago, I was not getting along very well with my wife. I had a very turbulent, but brief affair with my secretary. I realize now that it was a mistake, but I find myself dreaming about some of the experiences that I had during the affair. I have been known to talk in my sleep and I do not want my wife to find out about the situation with my secretary. My wife and I are getting along very well now and I do not want to spoil a good relationship. I also find myself not wanting to go to sleep at night, for fear that I will say something that I shouldn't.

                                      Signed,
                                      Sleep Talker

Dear Sleep Talker,

Obviously, for you, silence is golden. It would be foolish to admit your mistake to your wife, regardless of how you told her. Many people will agree with me on that point and others will not.

There is little to be known about dreams. And, anyone that tells you that dreams are important, is just "blowing smoke." Your dreams are a result of an over-reactive Subconscious. The Subconscious produces illogical and random thoughts during sleep and the information can only come from that information which is stored in the Memory Bank. The Subconscious is trained to send forward information that it, at present, does not yet have an answer for. You were trained to want to know WHY, and if the Subconscious has negatives stored that it does not understand, it will continue to send you those thoughts, possibly in the form of dreams. Because of the way you were trained, the Subconscious is just looking for answers.

Simply explain to yourself that the affair is part of your Past and that the Past does not exist. Explain to yourself that you do not talk in your sleep anymore and your fears will go away. The Subconscious Mind attempts to fulfill your suggestions. Also, before you go off to sleep, tell yourself that you dream only happy dreams and that you are happy and in love with your wife.

Dear Tom Ray,

I am going to graduate from high school in June and I would like to enter the field of hypnosis and become a hypnotherapist. What should I do to prepare myself to become a hypnotherapist?

Signed,
Young, Aspiring Hypnotist

Dear Young, Aspiring Hypnotist,

You should first get yourself a well-rounded college education. And, it would be even better to get a Master's Degree in some field. It makes no difference what you get your degree in, except that you should crank in a few behavioral science courses. Work at a variety of jobs, so that you can learn about people and how they react. The selling field is excellent for that purpose. Marry and have a child or two. The whole idea is to experience life a little, so when you are talking with someone, you can relate to common experiences.

After you have struggled out there in the world a few years, won some, lost some, possibly gone through the military and a variety of other situations and, in general, have lost your "wetness behind the ears," come to me and I will teach you how to be a hypnotherapist. While you are doing all those things, you should save your money, because I am going to charge to teach you!

LETTERS FROM MY RADIO TALK SHOW LISTENERS

Dear Tom Ray,

This morning, when you asked us to write a letter on a card, a piece of paper, a part of our shirt, newspapers, "anything," you convinced me to do it today. Fortunately, every Sunday morning, I have an opportunity to listen to you. My husband, our two children, and myself, throw a large paper route and I look forward to hearing your program.

Since I have started listening to you, many of the doors to my Subconscious have been opened. Now, as I look back, I have always had the key, but I didn't know how to open the doors with it. Last New Year's Eve, I quit smoking two packs of cigarettes a day. The way I quit this endless habit was through my Subconscious, as you explained on Sunday. Now that I know I can channel all my thoughts and energy to many good and positive changes, I will do so.

Once again, I look forward to and enjoy your program. On behalf of all your listeners, I would like to thank you for your care and your time.

> Signed,
> Newspaper Lady

Dear Tom Ray,

I just "happened" to tune in to your program this a.m. and feel that an unknown force guided me to turn the dial at that moment.

The subconscious and the unknown have always been subjects of great interest to me. I've been studying the subconscious and I do have some understanding of the subconscious; however, I have yet to learn how to manipulate the subconscious and how to surface my specific problems which are implanted so deep into my subconscious. I have yet to learn how to relax, which of course, is probably the first and most important step to begin the transition. As a result of being unable to relax, my entire back area is in constant pain from tension. Also, my conscious mind tells me I'd like to quit smoking, but my subconscious mind doesn't get the message.

I don't know anything about you, but I do know that your radio program was of great interest to me and I'm asking for your help. Not only for myself, but to teach my children at their young age before any negative concepts are allowed to be buried into their subconscious. And what better way to "spread the word" than by good example.

Please send me a tape or any brochure to steer me in the right direction. I have a good feeling that you can be of help.

Signed,
Uptight Dad

Dear Tom Ray,
I heard your broadcast this morning, for the first time in my life and I have never agreed with anyone more. Instead of thinking negative, I will from this day forward, think positive. I will start to teach my three sons the same meaning: whatever you feed the subconscious mind, it will accept. At the present time, my husband and I are in a situation that through your teachings, we are going to lick, mentally and physically. Because I know we are, if we feed our subconscious minds the good things. He doesn't have a job now. But he will get that job he seeks. We can't pay our debts now, but we will.

Please send me any brochures or literature that I

might be able to think positive. I feel great, fantastic, wonderful, and I am rich.

                              Signed,
                              Mrs. Rich

Dear Tom Ray,

    First of all, thank you for your show. I listen every Sunday morning. The information you have to offer is valuable to me, not only for myself, but it helps me with others, to understand and to relate to them. The first thing that hit home was your very first show on allergies. My sister-in-law who is 14 and lives at home with her parents has some problems with them that I think are of that nature. For one, she has asthma. When they lived in L.A. one summer, her parents let her stay with an aunt in Arizona, during which time she had no allergy problems. I think a good possibility that it was from not having the influence of her parents, who, by the way, get sick (colds and stuff) at the drop of a hat. So, they associated her good health to Arizona, and transferred that idea to her. They moved to Arizona, and she has been better. Although they go back to L.A. frequently (four or five times a year) she still had no problems. One time, we went to visit them for two weeks. My sister-in-law had some kind of ear trouble and saw a doctor. She had a small rupture in her eardrum. The thing that upset me was when I asked her to get me something out of the refrigerator, she said, "I can't. My mother told me to stay away from it." I said, "Why?" She returned with, "Because cold air comes out of it and I could catch a cold." I could have screamed! The thing is, what could I possibly say to her parents to let them know what they are doing to this girl? She's really beautiful and has so much potential and I see it being suppressed under her parents' over-protective wings. Any suggestions?

    P.S. I would like all of your booklets from day 1 and the relaxation tape please...Keep up the good programs.

                        Signed,
                        Concerned Sister-in-Law

Dear Tom Ray,

    I started hearing your program about a month ago. I am 16 years old. And I am fine, Thanks to God. And I do believe in God. I was brought up in Church. And I have always been a sick girl...(health). When it's not my earache, it's a toothache or a cold. And when you said that when you feel sick, you should say, "I am fine." (present tense) not, "I will be fine." (future tense).

    So, that morning, I had a bad cold. My eyes and head hurt. I had a stuffed-up nose, sore throat, and was sneezing. And at the same time, I had an earache. So then I prayed, and took your advice of telling myself I was fine. I looked at myself in the mirror and said, "I feel fine. There is no pain in me at this moment." I kept saying this for a couple of minutes. Then about 30 minutes later, I felt perfectly fine. No more pain! Of course, a sneeze, here and there. But, absolutely no pain. From that day on, whenever I get a toothache or something that makes me feel bad, I just say that I feel fine. And, it works!

                        Signed,
                        16 Year Old

Dear Sir:

I don't often listen to the radio, but last Sunday, I was searching for a good religious or educational program. Fortunately, I happened on the Tom Ray discussion on controlling emotions/actions/ performance through the suggestions to the subconscious mind.

I greatly benefited by Tom's teaching and commend your radio management for an excellent and helpful program. Please keep Tom Ray on your station and I will keep listening (with gratitude). Does he have a book or any written material we can get?

I completed a course in autohypnosis four years ago, taught by a Ph.D. in clinical psychology. Tom's explanations refreshed my memory and expanded the subject matter in a clear style.

Thanks.

Signed,
Seldom Listener

Dear Tom Ray,

I've written earlier, requesting the information you offered and am so pleased with the results, so far, of actually changing my thinking to change my life. I just had to write a progress report.

Mine is probably as typical a situation as exists today among divorced women with a family to support. I have been scared to death (past tense now) letting my fears of rejection and failure foster and control my ability to function and succeed in all areas of my life. My financial situation has really been in a strain. My former husband, being a successful businessman with his own set of values, hired a lawyer to limit the child support payments to twelve months (two years ago) in the actual legal divorce decree, stating any prolonged legal binding agreement could affect his business corporation and that he would continue the support just between us. I told myself that twelve months of legal support would give me time enough to balance out my income, along with the total emotional adjustment. After 12 months, since I did not know how to succeed, my income still needed the monthly support. Once the legal twelve months ended, any support was a result of threats, bribes, and a desire to have yet another "mistress" because I "owed it to him." Since last December, my life has been unbelievable. Behind all my pain and frustration was fear I could not seem to get rid of, until I happened to tune your program in the first Sunday morning you spoke over the radio.

Using your suggestions, I recently acquired a second job in sales, part-time, in addition to managing an insurance brokerage office during the day, and am confident my additional income will deliver me from the unfortunate situation. Thank you once again for your help.

Signed,
Divorced Mom

Dear Tom Ray,
It is so refreshing to hear someone taking the time to tell fellow human beings how to learn to control body functions! So often we hear only that one should do or not do this or that, but not how to.

Thank you for caring!
Are your past radio programs taped? They are priceless. You really have sense, and your instructions do work. I'm amazed and very grateful.

Signed,
Amazed and Grateful

Dear Tom Ray,
I am a first year medical student at the Medical School here in San Antonio. I am not normally up at 7:30 on Sunday morning, but I got up this morning to study for a test. I know that from now on, I am going to start listening to the radio on Sunday morning.

I am very interested in what you are saying and all that you have to offer, for I would like to try to incorporate your techniques into my practice someday.

Signed,
Medical Student

Dear Tom Ray,
I'm 13 years old, and I'd like to tell you that I really enjoy your program, and I hope you get to stay on the air. Last week, you had a really good talk on the subconscious mind. I thought about it a while and I agree fully that people can lead a much happier life if they would just think positive.

Anyway, I hope they don't take you off the air,

because I think it's doing a lot of people a lot of good!

Thank you for being there. Good luck and I'm going to keep listening.

        Signed,
        Young Student

Dear Tom Ray,

I heard your radio program this morning for the first time and I felt the urge to write to you. I will say I enjoyed what you had to say.

I have read a lot and studied about the subconscious mind, but as of today, I have not found a solution to my problem. Perhaps you can help me.

I had a thyroidectomy in 1954 and, since before that, as far back as 1941, my sleep patterns changed so drastically, I have not been able to sleep a free night in many years, without medication.

I have been to and am still going to a psychiatrist and have been going for years. They have no answers, but they all agree that I am manic-depressive and give me medication that does not help, most of the time.

I am doing good, if I sleep 16 hours a wcck. I know there must be an answer to my problem and perhaps you can help me.

This problem has persisted so long, it does make me depressive about it and I know the answer lies in my subconscious mind, but bringing it up front to where I can look at it, is something else and I'm in hopes you can help me with this. I've told myself many times, it's all in my mind, but I have not been able to deal with it, myself.

I would like to have the first chapter to your book. In fact, I would like to have the whole book and the steps as to how to get to the subconscious mind.

I feel that you can help me because of your understanding. I would certainly appreciate your relaxation tape. I think it would be of help to me.

Keep up your wonderful, worthwhile efforts and work. There just isn't enough understanding of the mind, even today.

Signed,
Sleepless

Dear Tom Ray,

I don't know if you remember me or not, but I wrote to you last week. I received your first chapter in the mail yesterday, and I have to admit, I was surprised. I wasn't too sure you'd have time to write. I enjoyed the chapter a lot.

This morning I got up late, and I only caught the last twenty minutes of your program. I agree that to have someone do what you want them to do, you have to let them know you appreciate them, but not what they're doing. My parents have always told me when I did something wrong, that it was very wrong, and they (only my dad) were pretty mad. My dad likes to yell, and he really lays it on me. I can't stand to be around him, and I wouldn't ever talk to him if I were having problems. I've tried before, but he doesn't care about anything that happens and he doesn't listen.

I wanted to ask you something. I have a problem when I'm talking. I have a habit of talking too fast, and, consequently, I slur my words. I'm doing a Christmas program at my church, and, unfortunately, I ended up playing the part of Mary. I know I'm going to have trouble, because during rehearsal, everyone keeps reminding me to speak up and slow down. I wouldn't know how to correct myself, because I don't hear myself the way other people hear me. If you have the time, could you please write to me and give me some advice? You don't know how much I'd appreciate it!

Thank you for your time and patience.

Signed,
Fast Talker

Dear Tom Ray,

My husband and I really do enjoy your program on Sunday morning. I only wish it were for a longer period of time.

The very first time I heard you speak was about a year and a half ago at a real estate meeting for Realty World agents. Leaving that night, I had such a positive attitude, it was incredible. Unfortunately, my attitude isn't always positive, which is my fault. Isn't that right? I realize these things, but have trouble practicing them.

I would be interested in receiving the first chapter of your book. I know reading anything written by you would be a real "feel-good." Keep up your good work. You're terrific!

Signed,
Real Estate Agent

NOTES

To Tom Ray,

The Final Revelation

The Lord is my Shepherd,
His Name is "I Am."
He giveth me bread,
And a smidgen of jam.

When I say, "I Am That,"
That's what I have become;
So I have the power
To be a Christ or a bum.

The Law hears my voice,
When it follows "I Am,"
And IT has no choice,
But to bless or to damn.

So I'll say, "I Am That,"
To all that is happy;
And "I Am Not That,"
To all that is crappy!

                    by Ophelia Ray

(A client of, but no kin to Tom Ray!)
Printed with permission from Ophelia Ray

TOM RAY'S TAPES FOR SALE

Description and List of AudioTapes. Each Cassette is only $10.00, plus $3.00 shipping and handling for 3 items. S & H for 4 or more is $6.00.

#101 STOP SMOKING

Most people are conditioned to think that smoking is a relaxing thing to do. When they try to give up this one thing that relaxes them, it is often a losing battle. When the Subconscious learns that you can relax without smoking, then it is very easy to put down the cigarettes forever. Some people say, "I enjoy smoking, but should quit for health reasons." People who stop smoking with the Hypnosis Science Stop Smoking Cassette find that they are not affected, even when exposed to others that are still smoking. Only $10.00! Order Now!

#102 LOSE WEIGHT AND KEEP IT OFF

If you could change your eating patterns and be happy, it would be very easy to lose that extra weight and keep it off. People overeat for many reasons. Some people don't even realize when they are overeating. Others think they don't eat too much, but still gain weight. The Hypnosis Science Weight Loss Cassette has proven to be very effective in helping overweight people that just cannot lose weight on their own. Only $10.00! Order Now!

#103 RELAX

Probably the one major cause of death today is tension. If everyone had been taught while in grade school to go to his Subconscious Mind and command his body to relax, the hospitals around the world would not be so full. This is probably one of the most misunderstood problems in the world today, yet one of the simplest to solve. Hypnosis Science Relaxation Cassette also teaches you how to deal with your Subconscious Mind from the waking state. Tom Ray's revolutionary word prescription is the answer to your needs. This cassette is a must in your library of self-help tapes. Only $10.00! Order Now!

#104 GET THAT JOB YOU WANT

Are you stuck in a job that you know is far less than you are capable of doing? Are you getting paid well for the work you are doing? Are you happy in your work? The Hypnosis Science Career Cassette will help you discover the real you and will release you to go on to bigger and better things. It is true that most of us have to work for a living, so why not enjoy the work that you do. Order this tape and see your future change for the better. Only $10.00! Order Now!

#105 BE A SUPER SALESMAN

Every salesman has the hidden talent to become a leader in his chosen profession. Before Tom Ray realized his talent in the field of hypnosis, he had been a super salesman with several different companies. You will receive subconscious suggestions based on actual past experiences, plus usable marketing theory that will help close that big sale. Don't accept "No" for an answer. Order the Hypnosis Science Super Salesman Cassette. Only $10.00! Order Now!

#106 SELF-HYPNOSIS

You have used self-hypnosis many times in your life, but you were probably not aware that you were doing so. The Subconscious Mind will accept your statements and thoughts literally. Unless you know how to go to the computer of your mind and program yourself for success, your time will be wasted. You should know how to stop pain, control blood flow and all of your body functions, so that you can obtain perfect health and keep it. The world is yours to have by controlling your body with your mind. This is an excellent tape for control of pain and disease. Hypnosis

Science Self-Hypnosis Cassette is a must for each and every person in the world today. Only $10.00! Order Now!

#107 FREE FROM ALCOHOL

When everyone realizes that a person drinks to relax, I think the world will be a better place to live in. When the Subconscious Mind experiences a drink, the alcohol has a calming effect. This, the Subconscious likes, and it says, "That felt good. I enjoy relaxing. Let's have another!" When the Subconscious Mind realizes that it can relax without the aid of alcohol, it determines that alcohol is probably too expensive and too much trouble, plus very unhealthy. I have seen 30-year alcoholics just give up the bottle after a couple of hypnosis sessions and still be able to enjoy a drink now and then socially. The Hypnosis Science Alcohol Cassette is a must for all drinkers. You will be amazed at the results. Only $10.00! Order Now!

#108 SEXUAL PROBLEMS SOLVED

Attitudes about sex seem to change much like the weather and, after a while, the Subconscious gets confused as to what to think. With the Hypnosis Science Sexual Attitudes Cassette, you can become comfortable with the idea that sex is a normal, healthy part of your life. If you have sexual hang-ups of any kind, this cassette will help. Only $10.00! Order Now!

#109 GET HEALTHY! STAY HEALTHY!

Continue seeing your doctor, but use your Subconscious Mind to repair your body and to keep it healthy. You are responsible for your own health! Get healthy and stay healthy with the Hypnosis Science Good Health Cassette. Only $10.00! Order Now!

(Copy this Order Form)   ORDER FORM

ITEM	DESCRIPTION	QUANTITY	UNIT PRICE	TOTAL
#101	Stop Smoking	*	$10.00	
#102	Lose Weight and Keep It Off	*	$10.00	
#103	Relax	*	$10.00	
#104	Get That Job You Want	*	$10.00	
#105	Be a Super Salesman	*	$10.00	
#106	Self-Hypnosis	*	$10.00	
#107	Free From Alcohol	*	$10.00	
#108	Sexual Problems Solved	*	$10.00	
#109	Get Healthy-Stay Healthy	*	$10.00	
#110	The Puzzle Factory Syndrome	*	$17.95	

                                (Texas Residents 8.25%)   **SUBTOTAL** _____
                                                                           SALES TAX _____
    $3.00 for 1-3 items $6.00 for 4 or more items   **SHIPPING** _____
    For large quantity discount: Contact Author   **TOTAL** _____

Name _____

Address _____   Send Order To:

City, State, Zip _____   GloTag Press

Payment Type (VISA, MC, check, MO) _____   P.O. Box 538

Credit Card Expiration Date _____   Pipe Creek, TX 78063

Signature _____

You can also order from: www.puzzlefactorysyndrome.com or www.thelawsofthesubconscious.com

"Speak Softly and Carry a Big Stick"

– Theodore Roosevelt, 26th President of the United States

"Yeah, so what's that got to do with the graphic arts?" Everything! Because like every business, some people can make what they do sound really great, but what they actually deliver is often far less than what they build you up to expect.

We prefer to follow the **"Theodore Roosevelt Principle."** Of course you can expect clear and concise communication from us, but the thing that speaks loudest is what we *deliver* – powerful, targeted graphic communication to reach your marketplace and enable you to make a return on your investment...after all, that's why you're doing this in the first place, isn't it.

Since 1985, Our firm has developed effective marketing communication collateral for a wide range of companies with diverse business profiles and sizes. Although the gamut of the companies we work with is very wide, they all have one thing in common – they love what we do for them and they choose to continue to work with us and refer their associates to us.

With us, "a Passion for Excellence" actually means something and it's not just an empty platitude - but don't believe me just because I say so. Ask our clients, they are the only ones whose opinions really matter. We'll be glad to give you a list of references upon request.

Need Help Growing Your Business?

Need a Great Company Brochure, New Corporate Identity, an Effective Web Site? Visit us online to see samples of what we've done for others. Like to see some printed samples? Contact us, we'll send you a sample packet. Have a question you would like fielded by an actual living breathing human being – give us a call, we'll be glad to help.

Getting ready to do something but you feel like you could be taken advantage of because of what you don't know? We have a *free publication** for you to help demystify the process and enable you to ask the right questions to separate the wheat from the chaff so you can make an informed, discriminating buying decision.

*FREE Information Publication

"Graphics & Printing Checklist"
Before you buy graphics or printing, this industry resource is a must read. Concisely written, it will arm you with the vital information you need to make an educated decision that's in your best interest. Download at: **www.masterpix.com/guide**

JASON ROBERTS & ASSOCIATES, INC.
GRAPHIC DESIGN • MULTIMEDIA • WEB

www.masterpix.com

7300 BLANCO ROAD, SUITE 606 • SAN ANTONIO, TEXAS 78216
(210) 340-2033 • TOLL-FREE (888) 899-4466